# To
# Present
# the Pretence

*Essays on the Theatre
and its Public*

'Twelve years ago I looked on at people's struggles, and wrote about them for the stage, sympathetically, but as an onlooker. Without consciously intending it, I have become a participant. These essays I hope will show how.'

This book is John Arden's own selection of his writings on and about the theatre over the past twelve years, complete with his own astute, provocative and nicely ironic commentary. Two of the essays are composed in collaboration with Margaretta D'Arcy, thus reflecting the dual nature of his work for the stage, which has included an impressive body of plays written together with D'Arcy (from *The Business of Good Government* in 1960 to such recent large-scale epics as *The Island of the Mighty* and *The Non-Stop Connolly Show*), as well as his own more personal work, such as *Live Like Pigs, Serjeant Musgrave's Dance* and *Armstrong's Last Goodnight*.

Here, then, is Arden on Brecht, Arden on O'Casey, Arden on Jonson. Here also is Arden in New York helping D'Arcy to mount a funny-serious pageant on the Vietnam War. Here, more sombrely, is Arden (and D'Arcy) on Ireland, and, finally, on Britain. The centre-piece is undoubtedly their jointly written exposition of the ideas, techniques and performance history of the fourteen-hour epic play on the life of the Irish Socialist, James Connolly, which was seen in Dublin in 1975 and, in single episodes, in London during the following year. Of equal stature is the text of a lecture on Playwrights and Play-writers given by Arden in Australia in 1975, and published here for the first time. There can be few other playwrights capable of such an analytical yet passionate approach to their own work and to the place of that work in the society for which it was written.

From the outset Arden is concerned with the basic function of theatre: 'The actor on the stage pretends: and presents the pretence to the public. To what end, and in what manner, the social conditions of the age and the occasion will determine.' It is precisely with the 'social conditions' of his own age that Arden finds himself increasingly concerned. He allows his readers, as the book unfolds, to follow his own development as a writer and to watch him change, as he himself says, from sympathetic onlooker to committed participant.

JOHN ARDEN

# To
# Present
# the Pretence

Essays on the Theatre
and its Public

(*including two essays written in collaboration
with Margaretta D'Arcy*)

*selected, with commentaries,
by the author*

Eyre Methuen
London

To my parents in their second half-century of marriage

J.A.

First published in 1977 by Eyre Methuen Ltd
11 New Fetter Lane London EC4P 4EE
© 1977 by John Arden
Printed in Great Britain by
Richard Clay (The Chaucer Press) Ltd, Bungay, Suffolk

ISBN 0 413 38150 1 (Hardback)
ISBN 0 413 38160 9 (Paperback)

# *Contents*

�

PART FOUR

*written in collaboration with Margaretta D'Arcy

# Acknowledgements

Acknowledgement is due to *Peace News*, 8 Elm Avenue, Nottingham, in which the following pieces first appeared (the *Peace News* title, if different, is given in brackets): 'Pasolini and Penn' ('Bonnie, Clyde and Jesus'), 'Some notes from New York', 'A First Class Texas Job', 'Not All That Representative' ('Uncomfortable Thoughts from New Sparta'), 'A Remonstration about Rhodesia', 'Politics and Prisoners' ('On Forbidden Ground'), and 'Politics and Police' ('Celto-phobia on the Euston to Holyhead Railway'); to *History Workshop, a journal of socialist historians*, 1 Rose Lane, Oxford, where 'A Socialist Hero on the Stage' first appeared; and to *Gambit – International Theatre Review*, 18 Brewer Street, London W1, where 'Ben Jonson and the Plumb-line' first appeared as 'An Embarrassment to the Tidy Mind'.

## Part One

✦

*Ancient Principles*

These essays were first written as occasional-pieces for various publications. Their arguments, as I discovered on reading them through again after a lapse of years, were not always as clear as I should have liked: so I have made some amendments, to eliminate ambiguity, and I have added the odd footnote. I have not materially changed the intention of any of the pieces. Of course, over the past twelve years, my views on various questions have undergone development. I have chosen for this collection those essays which seemed to best illustrate that development.

In some matters, however, I have not changed my mind. I began writing plays as long ago as 1946: and my first work to be performed was put together in 1954. It was Romantic Victoriana, about a farouche railway-navvy and an unprincipled upper-class maiden. It was based upon images from the old-fashioned Toy Theatre. If someone were to turn up the MS of this play and present it somewhere today, I would no doubt be embarrassed by its technical ineptitude, but I would not disown its fundamental conception. The art of the theatre is exceedingly ancient, and I do not believe that the principles underlying it have been radically altered by any of the innovations in style, adjustments to stage-practice, or shifts in the make-up of audiences which have occurred since the time of Thespis. The actor on the stage pretends: and presents the pretence to the public. To what end, and in what manner, the social conditions of the age and the occasion will determine. Sometimes the purpose is serious, sometimes frivolous: always there must be an element of the Doppelgänger about it. 'Look at us,' the players imply: 'We are you.' But the spectator well knows that they are also themselves, and they are also the figments of the imagination of the playwright. Their crucial combination of *pretence* and *presentation* gives rise to the strained, almost inhuman posture of the classic theatrical icon – those early nineteenth-century prints of actors in character – 'Mr Kean as Richard III' – 'Mrs Siddons as Volumnia' – one arm across the breast, the other stretched out, and the features contorted with apparently immobile passion. When I think of 'the Drama', it is always such an engraving with its crude primary colours and its tinsel embellishments that inevitably comes into my mind.

But to say this is to say nothing of the *content* of plays: what they tell, and to whom. To begin with, I was never very concerned about such things. I found a *story* which appealed to me, for whatever reason, and began to write it, in dialogue: and that was it. About twenty years ago, however, I entered into a working partnership with Margaretta D'Arcy (who has collaborated with me on two of the essays in this book). Her own instincts as a playwright have tended to operate in the reverse order to mine. She will think of a *subject* that requires to be dramatised: and will relate it to the conditions of the time and the potential audience to be sought for it. Only then will the idea of a story to embody the theme, and a style to narrate the story, become uppermost in her mind. The plays I have written by myself and those which she and I have written together are consequently, quite distinct, one group from the other, in both manner and matter. Nevertheless there are certain general ideas about the content of plays which we both hold in common. Let me illustrate what I mean by reference to the associated art of painting.

There is a well-known picture by Pieter Bruegel called *The Battle between Carnival and Lent*. It is basically an allegory of abstinence contrasted with over-indulgence; but there is a good deal more to it than that. In the crowded market-place of a sixteenth-century Flemish town what seems to be the entire population is assembled in order to dramatise, to themselves and for themselves, the passing of the Christmas feasting-season into the Lenten fast. Carnival, represented by a gross fat man with red breeches and a swollen cod-piece, sitting astride a barrel, jousts with Lent who perches on an angular upright chair. She is a sour female, lean, and armed with a baker's shovel containing two meagre fishes. He wields a spit loaded with meat and poultry. They are urged forward to the combat by their respective groups of supporters. Her chair is tugged on four small wheels by a priest and another thin woman. His barrel is pushed by two clowns in funny hats, with masked mummers beside them; while another fat man (or a boy dressed-up as a fat man?) wears a cooking-pot for a hat and offers them music on a sort of small guitar. On Lent's side of the square it is already Ash Wednesday. Black-cloaked religious people are coming out of church. Carnival has behind him a crowded Shrove Tuesday alehouse with drunkards and amorous couples thronging the windows to see the show. Near the church door a ragged barefoot woman, helped by a bent old man, pulls a handcart with what appears to be a corpse on it. Mutilated beggars, skylarking children, musicians, dancers, traders and miscellaneous inebriated revellers fill up the picture. The whole thing is an emblem of death in the midst of life: or, to put it another way, carnal life continuing despite the imminence of death. Tragedy: and Comedy: combined in the one image.

Because it is really an *emblem*, rather than the naturalistic genre-painting that at first sight it may seem to be, it is essentially theatrical in its form. All these people are *playing parts* which, taken together, add up to the complete allegory. Some of the parts they play are those of persons playing parts – the fat man in 'real life' is perhaps a butcher, and the lean woman keeps a fish-shop (or a bakery, for the feet of her chair are surrounded by biscuits and twists of unleavened bread): but they have been chosen by the painter to personify the persons who personify the protagonist and antagonist of the seasonal/moral drama. Within the main play of their enacted combat are three other subsidiary plays.

The first is on Lent's behalf, and takes place in the church. We can just see, through the open door, the holy images shrouded on the pillars. Their coverings will not be removed until Easter, when Christ will have risen and the world will be made new. Within this ritualistic 'stage-set', the curate, as a surrogate for God (if you like, an actor 'playing the role of God'), is hearing Confession and releasing his flock from the burden of sin. The Sacraments are defined as the 'outward and visible sign of an inward and spiritual truth' – a definition to be extended to Bruegel's painting itself and the whole art of the theatre in general.

The other two plays-within-the-play-within-the-picture are over against the alehouse where Carnival still hopes to prolong his doomed reign. One of them is described by art-historians as *De Vuile Bruid* or *The Dirty Bride*. It is presented by a group of actors performing in front of a primitive portable stage-booth made of a kind of tent propped up on poles. A male character with a rough wig and false beard is led by the hand to meet a woman, presumably the 'Bride', who comes out of the tent with her head bowed and a wide basket-hat pulled down over her eyes. It is not clear what should go on in the play beyond this, but the heavily-muffled postures of the actors – the eagerness of the man, the assumed submissiveness of the woman – imply the sexuality of the theme beyond need of a commentator's notes. Further back is another group of performers: we are told that their piece is *Valentine and Orson* – a story of the rightful heir to a kingdom reared by a she-bear in the woods. This may be so – there is no doubt that the tale was very popular in the middle ages, and indeed long continued a favourite subject in the traditional theatre right down to the Vincent Crummles era in the nineteenth century. Calderon's *Life is a Dream* is in some sort a variation of it – but the figure of the wild man (or wood-wose) was one which captured the imaginations of the time in many guises not necessarily linked to one particular chivalric romance. The actor representing him can be seen in Bruegel's market-place, wearing a suit covered with tufts of hair all over (to signify unkempt nakedness) and resting a huge club on his shoulder. He may be thought to indicate humanity cut off from God (the 'play' in the church), cut off from normal sexual relationship (the play of the Bride), and therefore, alone and menacing in his bestial ferocity, cut off from the whole main play of Carnival-versus-Lent which pretends to include him as a subsidiary side-show. The fact that this wood-wose is obscurely placed by the painter up in the top left-hand corner of the panel reinforces rather than mitigates against my interpretation. Bruegel was often inclined to under-emphasise crucial elements in his compositions (you have to search to find Christ in his *Road to Cavalry* or St Paul in *The Conversion on the Way to Damascus*): and there is anyway a clear diagonal to be traced from the wood-wose's feet, down along the cloak and stick of one of the beggars, past the left foot of a

man with his back to us crossing the square, to the very focal point
of the whole painting, where Carnival's spit clashes against the tip
of Lent's shovel. The opposite diagonal, significantly enough, leads
straight past the cart with the corpse in it to the open church door
and the curate at his work within. The picture is as it were balanced
between the wild man of the woods and the dwelling of God-made-
flesh.

One could go on at some length about the significance of the
'wild man': he crops up in early Celtic legend as Crazy Sweeney or
Mad Merlin, perhaps with overtones of pre-Christian animism; he
obsessed the artists of the Gothic middle ages, appearing on cathedral misericords and court tapestries; he takes on a socially-rebellious
persona in fourteenth-century England (Robin Hood or the Green
Man – with ballads and folk-plays to celebrate him and public-
houses named after him); he may, without stretching it too far, be
dimly discerned in some of the mid-twentieth-century transatlantic
mythology of the hippie, hairy, naked, unashamed, marauding and
yet gentle, scrying visions in his hasheesh and – so he hopes – 'sub-
verting' the social order. The social order, be it noted, includes both
Lent and Carnival: but the theatre can also in addition include –
*must* include, cannot indeed survive without – the wild man himself and the woods from which he emerges.

All this is by way of prologue to the first five of these pieces,
which are comments upon playwrights and film-directors whose
work I have particularly enjoyed, and who seem to me outstandingly
impregnated with various aspects of the tradition set out in Pieter
Bruegel's great panel. I should mention that the letter about Sean
O'Casey was written in response to a coldly derogatory obituary
notice in a London Sunday newspaper. All writers, I suppose, must
make their own lists of those colleagues, alive and dead, who form
for them the Jesse-tree leading back to what they take to be the
original loin-spring of their art. No two writers' lists, obviously, will
agree one with the other. But I think it is a duty incumbent upon
our craft to challenge unjust judgements about those whom we
admire, particularly when such a judgement is known to be widely
held and there is a danger of its becoming 'received'. In this age
of drama treated solely as literature and so studied at colleges for
the approval of examiners who wished it assessed in allegedly 'objective' categories, young people can be induced to ignore a good

playwright for the whole of their lives by a few ill-chosen words of denigration. A personal unscientific 'subjective' view of one's fellow-artists is therefore a necessary counterweight, and I hope it may do some good. I have deliberately not included any essays solely attacking the quality of anyone else's writing – not because I think that bad work should be let pass, but because I want this book to express my enthusiasm rather than my rejections. The things I reject will anyway be clear enough to the reader.

# Pasolini and Penn

*Legend and Reality*

1967

I have recently seen two films which both excited and disturbed me considerably. One was Pasolini's *Gospel according to St Matthew*, and the other was *Bonnie and Clyde* by Arthur Penn.

The apparent subjects of these two pictures have little in common. The first is a straightforward retelling of the well-known religious *legend* (for Pasolini deliberately makes no concessions to modern historical criticism of the Scriptures: he records 'St Matthew's' narrative, miracles and all, just as it was originally written), while the second is an account of a family group of small-time but, within their local limits, exceedingly dangerous American thieves of the early 1930s.

But, in its own way, the tale of Bonnie and Clyde is just as much of a legend as the life of Jesus. The ignorant, self-dramatising, unthinkingly brutal Clyde and his pathetic little mistress (a film-struck waitress from a rural snack bar who can conceive of no finer career than that of a gangster's moll) somehow contrived to impress themselves upon the imagination of the starving small-holders of the south-western states in the 'Grapes of Wrath' era as a kind of Robin Hood and Maid Marian couple (even to the extent of writing their own 'traditional' ballads for publication in the local papers, and also by their treatment of a police officer whom they catch and play jokes on in quite a Friar Tuck style).

They (apparently) did not give the money from the rich into the hands of the poor, but their refusal during a bank hold-up to pocket the savings of an old farmer would be more than sufficient to account for their reputation.

The film very successfully contrasts the 'legend' with the 'reality' by means of lightning changes of style, so that one understands that *both* aspects are equally true : hence, I take it, the unusual attention paid to the details of blood and wounds, et cetera, which seems to have upset some critics but which, taken in context, is essential to the meaning of the story.

I was reminded of a stanza in an Early English Robin Hood ballad which describes how the genial Robin and Little John, after a boisterous bit of greenwood horseplay (changing clothes with a monk to deceive the Sheriff, et cetera), cut the head off a little page boy 'for fear that he wolde telle'.

In rather the same way, Pasolini sets the miracles of Jesus on the screen so flatly and directly that one is forced to accept them as the sort of odd conduct which, though improbable, is perhaps not impossible, and which would certainly make the attitudes of both the people at large and the local politico-religious establishment understandable.

Also, the public utterances of the man are so provoking, if not arrogantly hysterical, that one's own attitude to his behaviour on the screen becomes ambivalent; I found myself identifying half the time with the Pharisees : yet the emphasis by the camera on the poverty and disease all around is a continual reminder that Jesus lived in an extreme situation. His extreme response to it was therefore not surprising and requires, even today, that one should urgently make one's own response with as little equivocation as possible (a requirement rarely produced by the reading of Gospels in church).

Arthur Penn, as well, emphasises the poverty and futility of the environment of his characters. The general conclusion of both films, taken together, seems to be that in such bad social circumstances some people will find nothing better to do than to become bank robbers, while others will be forced to declare themselves as heralds of some vaguely defined but, by contrast, clearly desirable 'heavenly kingdom', while others might yet do . . . what?

To me, however, as a dramatist, the most striking feature of these movies is the way in which they combine a scrupulous regard for what is said to have actually happened with a clearly conveyed knowledge of what the dramatis personae would have liked to have happened.

Clyde is both a sexually impotent killer *and* a romantic hero: Jesus is both a village carpenter gone-round-the-bend *and* the Son of God. The Crucifixion is both a routine Roman nastiness *and* an event of world-turning import: Bonnie with a machine-gun burst ripping down her body is both a lump of bloody human meat *and* a sister to Cleopatra, Mary Queen of Scots or Barbara Allen.

Penn and Pasolini, in their varied ways, have solved the eternal problem of realism *v.* romanticism, Ionesco *v.* Brecht, Shakespeare *v.* Shaw, politics *v.* art, commitment *v.* absurdity, or whatever you care to call it. Or rather, I think they have shown that it is not really a problem at all.

# Lorca and the Poetry of Stagecraft

## 1965

*Review of:*
Five plays (Comedies and Tragi-comedies) by Federico García
Lorca. Translated by James Graham-Lujan and Richard L.
O'Connell (Secker & Warburg).

Any persons who still hold that Lorca was not really a dramatist
but a lyric poet who never entirely came to grips with the requirements of the theatre (by which, I am afraid, they usually mean 'the
tricks and falsities of the old-fashioned commercial stage-craft')
should have a look at some of the stage-directions to these plays.

For example:

> *At the right appears the Sash Youth with hat as in Act One. He
> is sad. His arms hang at his sides and he looks at the Wife
> tenderly. If an actor exaggerates this character he should be hit
> over the head by the director. No-one should exaggerate. Farce
> always demands naturalness. The author has drawn the character
> and the tailor has dressed him. Simplicity . . .*

Or:

> *Don Perlimplin's room. At the centre there is a great bed
> topped by a canopy with plume ornaments. In the back wall there
> are six doors . . . it is the wedding night . . . Belisa appears,
> dressed in a great sleeping garment adorned with lace. She wears
> an enormous head-dress which launches cascades of needlework
> and lace down to her feet. Her hair is loose and her arms bare.*

(Let us continue this one to include some dialogue – I cannot resist it):

BELISA. The maid perfumed this room with thyme and not with mint as I ordered . . .

*At this moment there is a soft music of guitars. Belisa crosses her hands over her breast.*

Ah! Whoever seeks me ardently will find me. My thirst is never quenched, just as the thirst of the gargoyles who spurt water in the fountains is never quenched.

*The music continues.*

Oh, what music! Heavens, what music! Like the soft, warm, downy feathers of the swan! Oh, is it I? Or is it the music?

*She throws a great cape of red velvet over her shoulders and walks about the room . . .*

And then compare the direction in the previous scene. (The play is *Don Perlimplin and Belisa*.)

*The piano is heard. The stage is in darkness. Belisa opens the curtains of her balcony, almost naked, singing languidly.*

BELISA. Ah love, ah love.
Tight in my warm thighs imprisoned,
There swims like a fish the sun . . .

This writing is rococo and highly ornamental: and perhaps (some will think) unsuited for this reason to the stage: but a closer examination will show that there is not an image wasted in the dialogue and not one detail in the stage directions which is unnecessary to the director. Lorca, in fact, was working in that tradition of the theatre which came to him through puppet-plays (one of the pieces in this book *is* a puppet-play) and children's toy theatres, but which originated as far back as the Middle Ages, found its development in the Commedia dell'Arte, and took in, *en passant*, such writers as Shakespeare, Molière, and Alfred de Musset. Its north-western outlet was discovered by Synge – indeed, if one were to Hibernise the setting and speech-rhythms of *The Shoemaker's Prodigious Wife* one would have a complete Synge comedy. Plot: elderly husband quarrels continually with a young wife, who appears to seek other lovers. He leaves home in a huff, returns disguised as a ballad-singer – surely not puppeteer, as this translation curiously has it? – sings a song of an unhappy marriage and so works upon the wife that when he declares himself she agrees to take him back. Then they start quarrelling again.

The apparent simplicity of the stories of these plays is set against the suggestively rich imagery of their dialogue and the twopence-coloured décor to produce the genuine effect of peasant art – and yet they are not 'folksy', there is none of that tiresome bourgeois condescension which has made 'peasant' a cue for scorn these days. Lorca was able to immerse himself in small-town ways of life and thought, and at the same time to retain his own sophisticated awareness of 'high art'. *Don Perlimplin*, for example, belongs to the world of Mozart but it also has affinities with an old English popular play like *Johan Johan*. Lorca was able to mingle rustic humour (the joke of cuckoldry and the like) with a quite unanachronistic re-creation of the ideals of courtly love – which may be due to his being a Spaniard. *Don Quixote* has the same mixture.

Which brings us to a very moot point. Are these plays practicable for the English stage? Such productions of his tragedies as we have seen have usually been rather embarrassing. The comedies could be no less so. The reason is, I think, twofold.

(1) We have not yet found a way of training actors and (particularly) actresses so that they can divest themselves of their urban inhibitions and present lyrical passion without affectation. This can only be done at a much earlier stage than the drama school. As English education is now going from bad to worse the outlook is not hopeful.

(2) Unfortunately the translators do not help by providing a text written in a sort of stilted Hispano-American, which is frequently

far from 'speakable'. Take the first lines of the prologue to the puppet-play:

> Men and women, attention! Son, shut your little mouth and you, little girl, sit down, by all that's unholy. Now hush so the silence can grow as clear as if it were in its own spring ...

Shut your little mouth, indeed ...

# Sean O'Casey

## *A Letter to an Editor*
### 1964

I am rather sorry to find that Irving Wardle's obituary notice of Sean O'Casey follows the standard pattern for comments upon this dramatist. As I have been continuously inspired and excited by his plays – from all periods of his work – may I put forward the plea that his later plays are by no means as 'rancorous and rhetorically inflated' as Mr Wardle makes out?

True, they do appear so, if we make the false assumption that he was trying to write all the time in the same 'social-realist' style with which he began. But a play such as *Cock-a-doodle-dandy*, which happens to be set in the Irish countryside, only *happens* to be set there. As a picture of the life of that countryside it is demonstrably faulty; but, as a fertility comedy in roughly the medieval morality or even mummers' play tradition, it is surely psychologically accurate, poetically true, and about as rancorous as *Punch and Judy*.

O'Casey's exile caused him to write like a European rather than an Irishman. Opinions will clearly differ as to how 'local' we like our plays to be: but I think it is most important that future judgements of O'Casey's work should be based upon the understanding that his later writing was continuously experimental in form, theme and vocabulary.

The absence of complacency in the heart of an ageing writer is a sufficiently rare quality for it to need celebrating when it occurs: and if we are seeking rancour and inflated rhetoric we have only to look at some of the things said about the later O'Casey both in Ireland and elsewhere during recent years.

# Ben Jonson and the Plumb-Line

## 1972

I studied English Literature at school for an examination then known as The Higher School Certificate. There was a list of set books which was contrived (as I suppose such lists are still contrived) to contain at least one example of every important trend or tendency from Chaucer to T. S. Eliot: or, as the examiners would have phrased it, 'from Middle English to The Moderns'. Ben Jonson was not one of the authors included. We had two Shakespeare plays and a portion of *The Faerie Queene*: and then we jumped to *The Early Poems* of Milton. Shakespeare was studied in an atmosphere of 'The spacious days of Queen Elizabeth': Milton, on the other hand, was presented to us as the protagonist of 'The Puritan Revolution'.

There was a strong contrast implied between the bawdy and blood-boltered licence of the late sixteenth-century playhouse and the high seriousness of Christ's College Library – one imagined Milton, dressed in appropriate sub-fusc, heaving down great leather-bound theological and classical volumes from the shelves in order to extract his strongly moral themes; whereas Shakespeare, we were encouraged to believe, sat with a pint of sack in Burbage's dressing-room scratching hasty re-writes to *Hamlet* or *Henry V* while the stage-manager knocked impatiently on the door and Beaumont and Fletcher interfered with continual 'interpolations'.

I would not suggest that either picture is totally wrong. But at the age of sixteen I found myself a little puzzled by the extremely

arbitrary change from the one to the other. The gulf between them
seemed as great as that between the Bohemian Paris of *Hernani* and
the Victorian England of Matthew Arnold. Now the latter gulf is
explicable because it was at least geographical – the English channel
is still wide enough to prevent British and French writers getting
very close together. And French, of course, is not the same
language as English. But the lives of Shakespeare and Milton
actually overlapped within the same small monolingual city: they
must have had many acquaintances in common. Milton certainly
read Shakespeare – though his use of the dramatic form in
*Comus* and *Samson Agonistes* seems to belong to an altogether
different world from that of Falstaff or King Lear. What could
have been the artistic link? The answer is, in fact, Ben Jonson: and,
as I have already mentioned, Ben Jonson was omitted from the list
of set books. He was also, and perhaps for the same reasons,
omitted from the list of regular modern theatre repertories. He was
an embarrassment to the tidy mind.

Examiners have tidy minds, and so do theatrical managers. They
do not like dealing with writers who cannot be precisely 'placed',
whose works in performance do not come ready-equipped with an
easy traditional style of acting and presentation, who are not
clearly-defined as being the height of some particular literary or
dramatic 'movement'. The influences on Jonson were largely the
same as the influence upon Shakespeare (or on any other of the
playwrights of the period): and yet he did not make the same
use of those influences as did his contemporaries. Shakespeare seems
to have collected everything that he could from all the earlier writers
and then intuitively collated it to produce his own fully-formed in-
controvertible *magnum opus*. (Not for an age but for all time.)

Jonson collected in the same way: but instead of collating, re-
fining, and distilling some sort of magical essence, he erected his
material, block upon solid block, into a structure which he then
arrogantly announced stood higher than anyone else's.

And why not? Unlike Shakespeare, who apparently relied for
his classical lore upon Plutarch and Ovid (in translation be it noted),
Jonson was able to invoke the great names of Tacitus, Juvenal,

Horace, Sallust, Suetonius and heaven knows who, all read and comprehended in the original Latin and impeccably inserted – whole paragraphs at a time – into the matrices of his text.

But there were other items in the pile as well as these unimpeachable classics. Jonson no less than Shakespeare had come into the theatre as a hack-writer and script-cobbler. His earlier years there were impregnated with the aroma of the basic twopence-coloured repertory of the commercial stage. He wrote, for example, new scenes for *The Spanish Tragedy*: he scorned this popular work, and let everyone know of his scorn (which Shakespeare never did): but he was also deeply influenced by it. As a result of the Senecan furies of Kydd, Shakespeare wrote *Hamlet*: and there is no record of Shakespeare ever claiming that *Hamlet* is a work-of-art of an altogether higher kind than its source. But equally as a result of the same Senecan furies, Jonson wrote the Ghost of Sulla into his Roman tragedy *Catiline*: and remained obliviously confident that he was purifying and reforming the debased standards of the stage. Yet he lets this Ghost mouth all the traditional Marlovian/Kyddist threats of blood and disaster which for twenty years had filled the pit and disgusted the judicious. How did he manage to brazen out the contradiction? Simply because the *environment* of the Ghost was so regularly Roman that no critic could find fault with it. Quite otherwise with Shakespeare. Jonson himself had poked scorn at the amateurish and inadequate scholarship behind *Julius Caesar*. Had Shakespeare imagined he was making any sort of improvement upon the catchpenny barbarisms of *Titus Andronicus*? How could he have, when he blindly perpetrated such a line as 'Caesar did never wrong but with just cause?' Shakespeare seems to have taken the rebuke to heart, because the play was finally published with the offending verse rewritten. No doubt he appreciated the unwitting justice of Jonson's comment – the senators of *Julius Caesar* are rational political manipulators who have little use for such bombast. But had Jonson seen them that way? I suspect that his real objection to Caesar's 'Irish bull' was rather different. He had detected a piece of grammatic illogicality, and it made him laugh like a schoolmaster discovering howlers in a pupil's exercise. Traditional

Elizabethan hokum, such as Kydd's, was often thus ludicrous: therefore *Julius Caesar* was hokum. The essential realism of the play escaped him, because when he thought of realism in the context of Ancient Rome, he automatically thought of the Roman Authors themselves – whom Shakespeare could not read.

Catiline and Sejanus were to be realistic in this sense. In their speeches they might rant, so long as they did not breach the decorum of Latinate rhetoric: but there must be nothing anachronistic about the imagery or the stage-effects (no chiming-clocks, for example), and the structure of the plays must keep as closely as possible to Aristotelian rules. If the dialogue inspired laughter, it should only be because the character who spoke it was being satirised in the approved manner of Juvenal or Horace. Shakespeare's line from *Julius Caesar* would have done very well for one of Jonson's serio-comic monsters – his magistrate in *Bartholomew Fair* need not have been ashamed of it. But the first Roman emperor was a figure of awe – and a very correct Latinist in his own right. You might admire him, you might hate him, you must on no account smile at him. (That Shakespeare might possibly have seen through Caesar so far that he really did find cause to smile, and then deliberately chose to convey his mirth to the audience, was inconceivable to Jonson.)

It is here that we strike the main paradox of Jonson, the reason why we cannot fit him neatly in examiners' ticketed boxes. Jonson maintained, continuously and publicly, in print and in tap-rooms, that he was the first pure classicist in the English theatre. Now because Jonson was so sure of the necessity for this, Milton believed it: and when Milton wrote plays or masques he became more classical than Jonson, and presumably thought he was 'saving the drama from decay' even more thoroughly. But he wasn't: because he did not write for a vigorous public commercial theatre. Jonson did; and he was successful. Whatever his views on the demands of the box-office, Jonson's comedies filled it up with cash. In order to do this, his plays had to contain something more than pedantic obedience to Aristotle's book of rules. And that something was The Ghost of Sulla – it was traditional content within an academic form.

The form obsessed Jonson. He was determined, for instance, that his plays should be properly presented in book-form, with the characters and cast-lists accurately given, the scene-headings translated into Latin, the dedicatory epistles, prologues and epilogues all neatly in their place, and the text thoroughly gone over, revised and correctly spelled. I would guess that he also had quite a lot to do with the posthumous publication of Shakespeare's folio: it would be a duty to his dead colleague that he would feel obliged to fulfil: but one can well imagine the irritation with which he helped the actors sort through piles of illegible prompt-copies and alternative versions of different scenes – 'How can the theatre ever be taken seriously if writers will not trouble to look after their own scripts?' would be the keynote of his grumblings . . .

It is well known that Jonson was the stepson of a bricklayer and worked at that trade when he was a young man. I don't want to get too much involved in speculative biographical criticism here; but it does seem to me that bricklaying is very much the kind of early skill that one would deduce from the finished plays. A bricklayer needs to be patient and precise, his work is slow and repetitive, but every brick must be exactly laid (and brick after brick is a heavy business for the muscles). If one row of bricks is allowed to be set out of alignment because the worker is tired or lazy, then the whole wall gets more and more out of alignment as it goes up, until in the end one finds oneself with a sort of Leaning Tower of Pisa. A bricklayer who becomes a scholar and a poet is likely to be pedantic, heavy and over-conscientious.

It is not surprising to find that when Jonson wrote verse he set out the sentiment in prose first, and then turned it into metre. (A bricklayer would never simply start piling up his bricks one on the other – the line of his wall must first be marked out by pegs and tautened string, and as he works he must always keep his plumb-line and spirit-level handy.) But a bricklayer is not an architect – the design of the building has been made by someone else. A poet on the other hand has not only to build his play – he also has to determine what the play will say and through the mouths of which characters. Here Jonson becomes suddenly unexpected, and grotesque. His characters are monsters, their dialogue fantastical – though founded, as a good bricklayer's dialogue should be, on closely-observed idiom and everyday vocabulary (much more so than Shakespeare's – compare their respective Irishmen, in *Henry V* and *Bartholomew Fair*. There must have been plenty of Irishmen in London at that time: but where Shakespeare seems to have obtained a generalised impression of nationalist hysteria and boozy blasphemy, Jonson actually *listened* to every turn of phrase and noted it down).

The fantasy in the speech derives not from the words used but from the ideas conveyed: and Jonson's people can never stop piling ideas upon ideas until a kind of *reductio ad absurdium* is reached – he deliberately allows, in fact, his bricks to get out of alignment till the 'Leaning Tower' seems about to topple. And he controls it by two devices. First, each speech is very carefully assessed within the bounds of the scene of which it is a part, so that the fantasy never breaks the limit set by the structure of the play as a whole: and second, each character is rigidly fixed within the theoretical framework of the physiological Humours. Thus Sir Epicure Mammon is allowed to meditate upon what he will do with his riches when he gets them, until he sees himself – the great fat creature – striding naked among his paramours consuming, of all delicacies, the paps of a pregnant sow. But by the logic of the plot he is never actually allowed to do this, indeed he cannot do it, because he is not going to get rich, he is going to be gulled, and the audience knows it. The whole famous speech is that of an unbalanced manic hedonist whose debauches are purely imaginary.

But whose imagination? Whose mania? Sir Epicure's or Jonson's? There are many comic authors who could have conceived the argument of *The Alchemist* and carried it out with success. There is really no reason why Sir Epicure should not have contented himself with ordinary ambitions – a large country mansion, perhaps – the love of one courtesan – the employment of a French chef. He would have had his part in the play just the same and done just the same things in it.

The only other British author who handles human beings in quite this way is Dickens. Dickens does not pretend to be classical. But he does, much like Jonson, set himself up an unbreakable rigid plot and then – in the same authoritarian fashion – he curbs his characters to fit it. Where Jonson employs the control of a tight act-and-scene structure Dickens enforces discipline by means of undisclosed family ties – you suddenly find in the last chapter that Smike is the son of Ralph Nickleby and the whole *raison d'être* of Dotheboys Hall was to provide a typical Victorian skeleton-in-the-cupboard for the traditional miserly villain. Or so it appears – for we know perfectly well that Dickens, having once seen one of those dreadful Yorkshire schools, could not get it out of his system: but when he describes the school he must go on (in a kind of creative mania) to invent Squeers and I do not believe that Squeers' teaching methods were ever employed by even the worst illiterate schoolmaster that Dickens could possibly have met. ('How do you spell window? W-I-N-D-E-R ... off you go and clean it ...')

Because I was not taught about Jonson at school (oddly enough no novel by Dickens appeared in the examination list either) I had little notion what his plays were like. I tried, at the age of seventeen, to read one or two of them. I found them unreadable. Largely because of the accuracy of the idiom – it does need a glossary, where Shakespeare's more impressionist dialogue does not. But then – in 1950 – I went to see *Bartholomew Fair* at the Edinburgh Festival, directed by George Devine. The production was not, I recollect, particularly well received by the critics – they claimed to have been *bored* by either Jonson or Devine (they were not quite sure which – critics are commonly unable to distinguish between the production and the script unless the play is extremely familiar, and I don't suppose very many of them had seen or read *Bartholomew Fair* before). They used words like 'pedantic', 'heavy', 'over-conscientious'. This surprised me. There had, it is true, been a lot of long speeches, some of them almost incomprehensible: but the overall action of the play was so clear, the setting of the fair and its habitués so

precise, that it didn't seem to matter. I cannot remember the evening in much detail – the main impression I retain is one of having
actually *been at a fair* (rather than having seen a play about some
fictional people at a fair), and a fair full of very curious happenings
and juxtapositions of persons, which emerged, as it were, from out
of the crowd and then sank back into it.

There was a group of crooked horse-copers and con-men sitting
in a corner smoking churchwarden-pipes and muttering in some
obscure *argot*: there was a mad preacher sniffing his way sancti-
moniously towards the roast-pig stall with a gaggle of womenfolk
urging him on in a positive convoy of gluttonous lust: there was
one phrase of his – he allowed roast pig lest he be suspected 'of
Judaism, wherewith the brethren stand taxed': there was a lady
who needed urgently to relieve herself and was accommodated by
the roast-pig-woman with a frying-pan and the shelter of her booth.
There was, in fact, the whole of London, shuffling and prowling
about on the big Assembly Hall open stage – and each of them, one
way or another, as cracked as an old carrot.

To me, at that time, this was something very new in the theatre.
(I had had, it is true, a rather similar experience at Lindsay's *Three
Estates* in the same hall the previous year: but that play was such
an oddity anyway, being early Scots theatre, indeed almost the
only Scots theatre of international quality, that I had not really related it to my academic knowledge of the history of the British
stage). The experience I gained at *Bartholomew* Fair was one which
I had thought could only be obtained in the cinema. Plays, to my
mind, were normally a fairly small-scale business, which dealt only
with such notions as were absolutely demanded by the logic of the
plot. There was no doubt that Jonson's plot was thoroughly logical:
but logic, I thought, for a proclaimedly intellectual playwright
should not have included such a surrealist swoop as Zeal-of-the-
Land's parenthesis about Judaism. One knew that Puritans were
often absurd, and that a royalist Jacobean had good reason to dislike them: but surely he can never have met a preacher whose
moral theology was quite so arsy-versy?

Similarly the business about the frying-pan/pisspot was very low, was it not? Would Bergson have laughed? And at that time, re-member, I had a brain stuffed by schoolmasters with Bergson's Theory of Comedy – a theory which I did not find helpful, but which was – I understood – the kind of thing that serious classical playwrights wrote in accordance with ... Being taken short in a fair was quite simply a rude joke: and Jonson, if he had been correctly represented by himself and by the commentators, ought not to have indulged in it.

I determined, in short, that if I were to write social comedy, Jonson was the man to follow – though the critics in the national press that week were a fair warning of how such inconsistent stuff would be received. You had to decide whether you were an intel-lectual writer or a popular hack. If you were an intellectual you would fill your plays with very serious people talking very seriously and having *moral debates*: if you were a popular hack you could well bring in lavatory humour, and no one would mind. There was always the great example of Shakespeare for the popular hack – if he could do it: why could not a modern writer? But I could not find anything in Shakespeare in the nature of a craftsman's pattern-book. I was very much in need of a pattern-book, as I had already decided that no modern play was constructed in a way that I would care to imitate (I had not then discovered Brecht – who does in many ways resemble Jonson). Jonson, the bricklayer, could teach me how to lay my bricks in order. If I wanted to allow them to deviate now and then from the rule of the plumb-line, I would have to work that out for myself.

Which brings me to the conclusion that the kind of play studied under orders from academic tutors under orders from examiners are not the kind of plays from which a young writer will learn much of his craft. The plays that do not fit into the official cate-gories – *because* they do not fit into the official categories – are most probably the ones that will prove most useful. Büchner is an-other example. I studied German Literature for the same Higher School Certificate: and I never even heard his name.

There is one other aspect of Jonson I feel I must mention. He *said* some very good things. He talked 'scandal about Queen

Elizabeth' only a few years after she was dead: he boasted of having beaten his rival Marston in a brawl and 'taken his pistol from him': he claimed he would rather lose a friend than fail to break a good joke. The son of Sir Walter Raleigh, whose tutor he was in France, made him drunk and spreadeagled him in the street, telling the French Papists that this was as lively an image of the Crucifixion they were ever likely to see. Such a man cannot be dismissed, as Shaw attempted to dismiss him, as a mere 'brutish pendant' for he also went to prison for co-authorship of a seditious play: he could have got off (he had not written the offending lines), but he preferred to show his fellow-dramatists a degree of solidarity.

*Footnote ( 1976 ):*

Since writing the above essay, I learned something else about Jonson that needs to be borne in mind when we consider his character as a writer. At the time of the Gunpowder Plot (1605) he was a Roman Catholic convert: he seems also to have become an undercover informant for the secret police, reporting on the activities of those Catholics with whom he had social contacts. A number of the men on his list were executed for their part in the plot. The plot itself is now believed by historians to be (at least to an extent) the creation of government Provocative Agents. Altogether a most unsavoury morass of treachery in which to find an admired poet . . .

But look at it another way: Jonson's own way, presumably. (There are obvious modern parallels to the situation.) A writer who subscribes to a non-conformist ideology, and works in a Bohemian theatrical environment always just one step from the wrong side of the law, is bound to be acquainted with some rather 'peculiar' people. Suppose him to discover that a group of these people, in pursuit of what he himself believes to be an entirely legitimate political end ('Civil Rights for Catholics') have got themselves caught up with an insanely adventurist programme of sabotage and mass murder, from which he can foresee no conceivable benefit to their cause in particular or the community at large. Furthermore he discovers that the existence of a plot is known to the authorities, though not in precise detail. The government wants names. If the right names are not provided, some monstrous pre-emptive pogrom may be set afoot against every Catholic in England. To give information, under these circumstances, might seem less a betrayal of some of his friends than a means of protection for a great many others whom he knows not to be implicated. He also presumably knows that he himself is manipulated by unscrupulous police blackmail: but what else can he do?

We cannot *judge* Jonson, because the records tell us so little of what really took place: but it is obvious he must have suffered the most traumatic conflict of loyalties. We would naturally expect to find this reflected in his work. The scale of his dilemma was surely Dostoyevskian. Had it happened to Shakespeare, what would we not have looked for from the creator of Lear and Timon? What we get, of course, from Jonson, is the allusive parable *Catiline*, written several years afterwards, cold, hard, correct: emotions manacled, one might say, in the iron clamps of 'objectivity'. The convention of Sulla's Ghost transforms the real-life conversations with Catesby and perhaps Guy Fawkes into a strange mixture of classical hyperbole and theatrical pomp. Cicero, who stands for Cecil, the chief minister of King James, is given great chunks of his own orations to utter, translated into English verse – from one point of view a natural dramatic tactic for a consciously learned playwright: but is it not also a most convenient technique for cooling the story down with the dry draughts of remembered classrooms? The horror of the plot is emphasised – hints of *gunpowder* in Ancient Rome are dropped, but never so directly as to form a Shakespearian anachronism – and the inner conflict of the informer is, as it were, passed over (i.e. if the villainy of Catiline is already shown to be so fearful, why should the audience imagine that a man need have qualms about revealing it to Cicero?). Whatever he might have felt deep down inside, the one thing Jonson would not do was to lay open the turmoil of his conscience on the public stage. Plumb-line and spirit-level control all.

Jonson was opposed to Puritans. Playwrights of the period commonly were, because most Puritans opposed the stage. But in his rigid refusal to allow his own emotional history to take precedence in *Catiline* over the fundamental issue of 'the Preservation of the Republic', we can see just how close he came to the grim stoicism of *Samson Agonistes* . . .

# Brecht and the British

## 1964

*Review of:*
Brecht on Theatre, translated by John Willett (Methuen).

A dramatist who takes his work sufficiently seriously to compile a whole series of theoretical essays about it is an un-English and (we may think) an untheatrical phenomenon. When the essays in question are written in the peculiar and untranslatable style of German philosophy, full of perilous abstractions and portentous statements which appear to mean nothing to the 'average practical man of the theatre', one is not surprised to find that they carry comparatively little weight in this country, except among a few dedicated actors and producers.

The 'correct' attitude towards Brecht's theories is to say – 'of course he was a marvellous director, but we should not take the ideas seriously – he had to write all this heavyweight stuff in order to convince the Germans that he was in earnest'. There is some truth in this: I have been told by a man who acted as his assistant for some years in East Berlin that Brecht often enjoyed a laugh at the expense of people who quoted his theories pendantically against him, and that he was always ready to contradict his own stated ideas in practice if the exigencies of the theatre appeared to demand it. But this is not the whole story. Brecht was passionately concerned that the theatre should be something far more than a place of entertainment in the sloppiest sense of the word. He believed that it was a potential instrument of social progress; and that the playwright, by reflecting in his work the true image of human society, assisted the members of that society to diagnose the defects in the image and thence to improve the reality out of all recognition.

Now this is in no way an ignoble role for the theatre. Why then has it met with such opposition in this country? Why should we assert *with pride* that we cannot understand Brecht's theories? Is it really a matter for congratulation that the English theatrical profession has no use for a man who has called on us so clearly to be of some use ourselves? First, of course, there is the unfortunate fact that Brecht was on the 'wrong' side in the Cold War. There are many excellent people, by no means McCarthyites, who cannot bring themselves to accept that a man can be a Communist – and the subsidised servant of one of the most rigorous and doctrinaire Communist governments at that – and yet can set us right time and again upon issues where he is correct and we are demonstrably wrong. Hence the various efforts to show that Brecht's Marxism was at best opportunist and at worst insincere. But granted that there was much of which he must have disapproved in the conduct of the Ulbricht administration, it is surely inconceivable that an artist of such stature could have continuously maintained a political allegience as a sort of public untruth. Brecht was a Marxist: but he was also a realist and was well aware that the East German Government had come into being, not because the German masses had successfully carried through the Revolution, but because the Red Army had destroyed Hitler and occupied the land. He was not so foolish as to believe the New Jerusalem to be instantly and flawlessly manifest. Clearly Marxist rule, under such circumstances, must bristle with anomalies. But he saw no reason therefore to abandon his faith in its theoretical possibilities and its ultimate fulfilment. To expect him, because of the riots of 1953 for example, to defect to the West is like expecting a Catholic to turn Protestant solely because of the scandalous life of a Pope, or contradictions in the doctrine of birth-control.

But even if Brecht had not been an East German Communist, I cannot think that his ideas would have had any greater impression upon our theatrical activities. To start with, he asks far too much from actors and producers. The amount of work – sheer dogged attention to detail – that goes into any production mounted at the

Berliner Ensemble is impossible to imagine in any English theatre
that I can think of. This is partly a question of economics: when
the State does subsidise our stages, it never gives enough, and so
there is never enough time or space to ensure that everything that
ought to be done is done. But I have seen a theatre in *West* Berlin
nearly as rich and secure as the Ensemble, but where the morale of
the staff is low and the work presented is comparatively perfunctory.
Why? Because, with one or two discontented exceptions (and those,
old disciples of Brecht) the men responsible are not possessed by
any ideological purpose – they see a play as a show to be presented
for its superficial attractions and if anyone suggests that it might
hold a deeper meaning, they will shrug their shoulders – why
bother, the audiences won't want it anyway ...

I mentioned above the awkwardness of Brecht's theoretical style –
in translation. What are we to make of a paragraph that reads:

'The old A-effects quite remove the object represented from the
spectator's grasp, turning it into something that cannot be
altered; the new are not odd in themselves, though the unscientific
eye stamps anything strange as odd. The new alienations are
only designed to free socially conditioned phenomena from the
stamp of familiarity which protects them against our grasp
today.' ...?

This *is* difficult, but it is also important. I take it as meaning that
whatever is shown upon a stage, whether people, objects, or events,
must be shown so precisely, so clearly, so transparently indeed,
that it seems like a *new thing*: only then will the audience be able to
understand its significance for their own lives – a moral, social,
political significance which implies possibility of change, and which
they ignore at their peril. (Thus Aristophanes in *Lysistrata*, to a city
weary of war but apparently hopeless of ever ending it, showed
that half the population* – the women – had never been consulted

---

* After I had written this phrase I remembered the large numbers and
economic importance of the slaves in ancient Athens. Should I change
it to 'half the *free* population'? But could one describe the women of

about the war in the first place. This was a social circumstance that all Athenians 'knew', but had so taken for granted that its revolutionary possibilities remained entirely hidden. Aristophanes exposed them: his play was disregarded: the Athenians suffered . . .)

The ignorant acceptance of wrong situations that can be put right is the main enemy that Brecht set himself to fight. He understood that traditional bourgeois theatre existed to maintain the status quo. Marx called religion the 'opiate of the people', Auden called commercial cinema a 'vast contraceptive', and to Brecht the true theatre was neither of these: it was a workshop where every worker was independently and communally dedicated to the construction of an image of society that should express both the fallibility of humanity and also its potential majesty.

All the involved and tortuous arguments in this book eventually reduce themselves to this over-riding principle. (His words are not always tortuous – in the plays they never are – but he was writing his essays for professionals of like mind to himself, and they must be judged on that basis.) However difficult the theories may appear to be, when they are fully understood in terms of theatrical practicality they are found to be always directed towards the pleasure and understanding of his theatre audiences. The word *Spass* (fun)

---

the age as in any way '*free*'? Should I encumber my paragraph with an awkward construction like, 'as many persons again as those who held fully-enfranchised citizenship'? I decided not to bother: but it is none the less worth pointing out in a footnote that if Artistophanes ignored the possibility of a servile as well as a female revolt it would not have been because of its implausibility. It was in fact a more probable happening in a depressed city-state than the sexual strike which he describes (though not necessarily more suited to the comic stage). No doubt the idea did not amuse him: it would have been rather too dangerous. The insight of even the most perspicacious writer is always thus limited by the conditions and prejudices of his time. The methods of a poet like Brecht cannot be expected to eliminate these barriers. But to follow his methods is to become ever more aware of the *existence* of the barriers. Once we have discerned them we can then seek the means to surmount them or to break them down.

crops up time and time again. Brecht never forgot that the theatre must entertain: but he knew that entertainment in the fullest sense means more than whiling away two or three hours in undemanding pleasure: it also means the improvement and enrichment of our understanding of life. I recently saw two shows in East Berlin. One, at the State Opera, was a stupid Stalinist opera about a Red Air Force pilot who lost the use of his feet and yet continued flying. It was complacent and crammed with received ideas. It was monotonous on the stage and did not once astonish its audience. It was certainly well-performed, and the public were respectful. They were in no way entertained. Revolution, and Anti-Fascism were invoked in the script (and in the programme-notes) as unexamined code-words to show that the authors were in the approved camp. The British film about Douglas Bader had an identical fable: the patriotic ideals for which its hero fought were not quite the same: but they were equally 'codified' and equally unscrutinised. The Brecht play, on the other hand – *The Days of the Commune* – was impregnated with youth, hope, enthusiasm and humour. It was light, and delightful simply to watch it happen, tragic though the conclusion of the fable was to be. It emphasised the unpredictability of human beings, their refusal to respond like Pavlov dogs to every meat-headed decision made on their behalf by those in power. Ostensibly a tribute to a bloody-minded city which defied the bourgeois capitalists a long time ago, it was also an implicit warning that a government need not be capitalist to betray the trust of the people: errors and crimes can be committed by uncontrolled persons of any ideology: Berlin (1953) was much nearer to that audience than Paris (1871).

# Part Two

*The Matter of Vietnam*

Was there perhaps a note of apology in the essay on Brecht for his being so openly and unrepentantly 'political' – political in the sense of adhering deliberately to one particular doctrine and the party that embodied it? 1964, when the piece was written, was the height of 'The Swinging Sixties', with Libertarianism (if it comes to that, Libertinism) the main social creed of the publicly aware artist. The international Communist movement, not so long relieved of the Minotaur-like J. V. Stalin, had been singularly unable to persuade the new generation of radical spirits that the Labyrinth in and over which he had brooded was done away with when he died. People were legitimately outraged by what had happened in Hungary: and any sort of doctrinaire disciplined party-structure was angrily deprecated. The world was about to be changed by huge public poetry-readings, non-violent anarchism, mixed-media, and topless dresses. We despised Harold Macmillan for having informed us we had never had it so good – he told us the truth: there was a boom-economy: the arts lived high on the hog and vehemently protested against their own affluence. The war in Vietnam was but a cloud like a man's hand: the enormous demonstrations on behalf of Nuclear Disarmament testified at once to our good intentions for the human race and our ironic assurance that Britain still was and would remain a world-power – admittedly not in the same class as the USA or the USSR: but, like them, still concerned to wage major war at 'high density'. The world-wide pattern that was slowly to emerge of guerilla campaigns, counter-insurgency operations, 'destabilisation' of inimical governments, electrocution of

suspects' genitals in vomit-spattered police-cells, murder-squads
prowling the suburbs by night and suicide-squads on the sky-jack
with gelignite strapped to their stomachs – all this was as yet largely
concealed from our comprehension . . .

As the decade progressed, and Labour government began to remind us more and more of the lessees of a sleazy restaurant who
must pay protection-money to LBJ and his neighbourhood mobsters
(in fact the theme of a play I was to be involved with in '68*), the
casual flower-power aroma of our pacifism began to fade away.
*Peace News*, for which in these years I wrote a column and several
feature-articles, determined quite suddenly that both sides in the
escalating Vietnamese conflict were not equally wrong (the hitherto
orthodox non-violent position): but that the Communists were less
wrong than the American democrats. Should Harold Wilson in
fact have sent troops to coerce Rhodesia . . .? We can now guess that
he couldn't have. They would not perhaps have mutinied exactly:
but their general-officers would have found sound reasons for 'dis-
suading' him, as in Ulster in 1914, as in Ulster in 1974, – see page
136 . . .

Margaretta D'Arcy and myself went to America for a few months
in 1967. My account of what we did in the Theatre Department of
New York University was written soon afterwards as a kind of
spoof – not because we did not regard our project there as a serious
one, but because the whole hysterical experience seemed at the time
beyond rational analysis. In order to avoid, on the one hand a
goody-goody self-congratulatory catalogue of our own virtues in producing what was after all only a one-day unscripted under-rehearsed
attempt at something new – or, on the other hand an assessment so
depreciatory that it would seem as though I thought we had made
no impact at all – I approached the event in the pastiche frame-of-
mind of a right-wing reviewer for, shall we say, *Time* magazine.
The result it that it is now hard for me to remember how much of
the article is true and how much a figment of my imaginary *Time*-
man's defamatory venom. Certainly the various professorial figures
referred to in the piece would be unlikely to recognise their conscientious selves if they were to come upon it today : but (on the off-
chance that one or other of them may be thinking of laying it before
lawyers) I here and now unequivocally affirm that there is no known

* see page 83

connection between Dean Corrigan and Alger Hiss, that Professor Hoffman could not possibly have been as old as 83, and that neither of them was observably losing his hair in 1967.

None the less, whatever the immediate artistic value of the *War Carnival* – and a number of people in New York still remembered it when I revisited their city in 1976 – it did prove to be something of a turning-point in my career as a playwright. The overall concept of the show was due largely to Margaretta D'Arcy, who was not officially employed by NYU at all. I had been hired as a lecturer to begin with: when I took up the post I was also asked to conduct a group of students in whatever project suggested itself. I agreed, on condition that D'Arcy would be formally associated with me on all *practical* work, this being rather outside my own professional experience, whereas she was already well-seasoned as a performer and experimental director. Personally I had small notion of what could be done with these students. But some members of the class had read a loosely-conceived suggestion I put forward in connection with my play *The Workhouse Donkey* – that it ought to have been extended to day-long continuous performance, interspersed with all sorts of thematically-relevant interludes. It was offered me as a challenge by these students: could it actually be done? Moreover, the class was very troubled about Vietnam and wanted to tackle the matter of war as part of their college theatre-work. D'Arcy (excited *en passant* by some of the other classes in the Department – circus-techniques, games-theories, et cetera) declared the practicality of containing both ideas in the one show and actually *presenting* it within our very limited space of time.

If I had been left to myself I would almost certainly have drifted and dithered and in the end produced nothing of any great consequence. I was then, and indeed still am, retrogressively inclined to take refuge in the comforting concept of the 'perfected script' before I dare put one of my ten toes into the deep water of active stage-craft. I have a horror of the extemporary buried deep in my sub-conscious, while consciously I understand that – in the present age at any rate – spontaneous ensemble improvisation is perhaps the only force to jerk the theatre forward from the successive ruts in which it sticks year after year. Of course it would have been an advantage to have had enough time to sit down and write out the

complete *Grandma* cycle, once its essential shape had been improvised by the group. But then, if we had done that, LBJ might
have retired, Nixon been disgraced, and Kissinger's diplomacy
foundered in Indo-China long long before any performance could
have been made ready.

It was D'Arcy who got in touch with all the external groups who
took part in our *Carnival*. Indeed it was solely her idea that external
groups should be brought into it at all. She thus began a series of
contacts in the avant-garde or 'fringe' theatre which we have never
relinquished, and which have virtually kept us alive as dramatists
when the more formally-organised subsidised theatres have been
unwilling to accept our notions (or, as they would perhaps have it,
our personalities). The following year, for instance, she was to be
unofficially instrumental in bringing over to Britain the Bread and
Puppet players, and when their arranged booking at the Institute
of Contemporary Arts failed to draw the type of audience they
sought, she found them another locale with Ed Berman at the
Kennington Oval. During our American stay she travelled to San
Francisco and met the SF Mime Troupe, from which a number of
actors were later to come to see her in London, where they introduced certain hitherto hardly-known concepts of street-theatre. She
also materially assisted the La Mama Company to undertake its
first European tour.

I mention these circumstances because I think it is high time to
clear up a number of misconceptions that have grown around my
own alleged initiatives in what is called 'community theatre'. I
have in fact never taken any, except on paper. On paper in the
mid-sixties, I was a militant war-resister and an activist of the
Committee of 100, perpetrating civil disobedience at every flourish
of my coffee-cup. There is no doubt that I approved of these activities: but my actual physical association with them was strictly
limited. Similarly, when unorthodox theatre-work has been called
for, I have gone along with it; and once told what is expected of
me, where I am to stand and move, what sort of reeling and
writhing and fainting-in-coils I am to indulge in, I have been able
to contribute I suppose as much as anyone to the finished product.
But I do like to be able to relate it to what younger and more

mobile minds might think of as 'straight theatre'. If I can discover, for instance, that a particular staging arrived at by communal consensus for a street-play or a piece of agitprop was anticipated in Vicenza by a Renaissance Commedia Troupe, I know exactly where we are, and can happily carry on. This is probably not the kind of relevantly meaningful audience-related structuralism which is supposed to be the mainspring of this sort of aesthetic ... Does it matter?

As Brecht said somewhere: 'if it works, it works'.

The *sine qua non* of all theatre-work is that the audiences should be continuously entertained and invigorated: by 1968 it had become apparent that the regular theatre for which I had written most of my plays was no longer an adequate medium for this. The so-called *revolution* at the Royal Court and Theatre Workshop in the late fifties had been largely a revolution of *content*. Playwrights were at last handling a whole range of material hitherto unacceptable to critics and managements, to say nothing of the Lord Chamberlain. The response to the taboo-breaking of Osborne, Behan, Delaney, Wesker *et al* proved that there was an audience for such plays, an audience which had been growing more and more frustrated with the fare served up to it through the previous decade. But this new (or renewed) public was still expected to submit to exactly the same actor-audience relationships which had obtained at least since the start of the century, when the Royal Court Theatre was only the Court Theatre, and George Bernard Shaw and Harley Granville-Barker were the latest New Wave. The structure of theatre-management and the status of the playwright within it had scarcely altered a jot, despite all the attempts made by the late George Devine to 'bring the writers into the theatre'. His ideas on this subject affected me radically: but when he died they seemed to have affected few others – particularly few among the directors, of whom more later.

Nevertheless, even after my visit to New York and all the innovations I found there, my objections to 'regular theatre' remained primarily aesthetic. Plays presented according to normal practice were lacking in essential impact: there must surely be some far more 'electrical' method of putting the stuff across ... That an attempt to achieve this was bound of its very nature to involve serious political difficulties within the social set-up of the theatrical profession itself was not at first apparent. At this time my only concept of *political* drama was one of *plays written upon political subjects* : and I was concerned only to improve the conditions under which such work could be set afoot . . .

# Roll Up Roll Up to the Carnival of War!

## 1967

America's determination to win in Vietnam, boosted by balding gangrenous General Westmorland's (97) flying stop-over to West Point and Congress, grows no less. Coincident with such inspirational escalation, however, the moans and wails of the Vietnik hoodlums continue to increase the decibel count of the Union. Latest in such unlicked bearcub protest was the 13 May actfest in New York University's new 300-odd capacity theatre – endowed largely through cultural foundation grants with the aim of establishing an all-American powerhouse of dramatic art. Not hitherto remarkable for treason, NYU boobed when it invited Britnik playwrite John Arden (beatle-haired balding pushing 37) and his frantic consort, mini-skirted teenage Margaretta D'Arcy (admits to 26, declares to press 'Call me an anarchist agitator'). Arden was expected to accustom NYU theatre students to impact of 'British New Wave' notions of drama, and, initially allotted one two-hour seminar per week, meekly accepted his academic role. Or so it was believed. NYU's Dean of Fine Arts Robert Corrigan (balding blond Alger Hiss-type liberal) had not bargained for the influence of sexy mother-of-four Miss D'Arcy. Arden's third seminar reeled when she launched into an unprecedented attack on the War, the University, the Students, LBJ, and such un-British aspects of our way of life as race-riots,* Cardinal Spellman, tax-paying and

* She forgot Notting Hill, London (1958) and Smethwick (1964), both Britannic contributions to world colour-tensions.

imperial responsibilities. 'You want to act,' she screamed: 'So act against the War.' Brainwashed students promptly agreed and the War Carnival was launched.

## In line with Mao

Arden, heretofore noted mainly for such portentous academic soul-dredgers as *Serjeant Musgrave's Dance* and *Armstrong's Last Goodnite* (Shakespearian bromides of a pessimistic pattern geared to Britain's reduced global power), complied with activist student demands that his new work should last all day and contain no climax. This was no more than in line with Chairman Mao's famed 'cultural revolution' wherein teenage demonstrators occupied Chinese sidewalks from sunrise to sunrise never letting-up on their slogan-shouting: but to NYU's balding gnome-like theatre-school Professor Ted Hoffman (83) it seemed likely to strain college resources to the outmost. An abortive attempt by Hoffman (nervous of damage to life, limb and University property) to cut down on the project budget was foiled by Miss D'Arcy who brought into play leftish hysteria, hailed Hoffman as a 'running dog of the CIA' and a 'tiresome little man'* Hoffman, not yet able to distinguish artistic enthusiasm from hard-core subversion, caved in. The War Carnival was planned to centre around a so-called Game, wherein members of the audience were compelled by rabble-rousing 'recruiting-sergeants' to enlist in one of two armies, distinguished by dabs of coloured greasepaint on their foreheads. The dabs were red or green, presumably in reference to Commie Viet-Cong and our own Green Berets, though neither side was distinguished as being better than the other – thus demolishing in the first half-hour any pretence of objectivity.

## Navel of a nude

Before the sides were selected the theatre had presented the semblance of a Carnival (in British parlance, a 'funfair'): games of chance – tossing rings over pegs, throwing balls at the navel-

* Swinging-London argot for rat-fink. Miss D'Arcy is Dublin-raised.

aperture of a life-size painting of a nude woman, etc. – were in full swing when an apparent quarrel between two students erupted into a full-scale rumble and with a yell of 'My God he's dead' 22-year-old redhead Jennifer Merin (student actress) flung herself over what seemed in all truth to be the lifeless corpse of one of her class-mates. Immediately three stilt-walking actors, garbed as Oriental war-gods, made their appearance, sending a chill through the audience, and Arden began a long funeral-oration-type speech, ending with a call for 'Peace'. Peace in his Moscow-directed vocabulary meant of course War, and within two minutes the entire theatre was reverberating to reiterations of 'Peace, Peace' – the audience, who were not confined to the banks of seats but spilled about a wide floor-area with no formal stage, found it only too easy to participate in such mass-hysteria, and were pushovers for the grim 'enlistment' episode which followed. While the armies were assembled, film (obtained by subversive subterfuge from US Army sources) was projected on a backcloth, showing such evocative scenes as the enrolment and basic training of American draftees. An unpleasant overtone was given when clips of Nazi film-stock of similar (German: 1939) happenings were included for the audience to make the obvious and libellous connection. Only too many of the pre-conditioned Peacenik element did indeed make the connection.

## The Russian, predictably, won

The Game itself – to the accompaniment of militaristic drum-beats from percussionist Herb Harris, who sweated, balding and 76, at his tympani from 2 pm till long past midnight – consisted of the two armies marching round and round a marked out race-track until stopped by a blast on the MC's whistle. MC Omar Shapli (Egyptian born, moustache-wearing, Com-symp acting-teacher whose theatrical notions derive from seasons spent satirising the West in Chicago's 'Second City' cabaret) had previously supplied each participant in the Game with a placard denoting his or her presumed racial and professional characteristics — e.g. 'Talkative Polish Monk' or 'Happy Negro Pimp' – and at each break in the march-around two players were selected arbitarily to stage a confrontation. Shapli issued the rules for the confrontation, compelling the pair to engage in such verbal contests as 'Make up proverbs, first man to falter is dead' or 'Construct a rhyming poem, alternate lines to each player, first man who drops meter or rhyme-scheme is dead'. When verbal invention flagged, physical confrontations were introduced, thus a 'One-legged Dutch Sailor' was forced to run a race with an 'Athletic Russian Interpreter'. The Russian, predictably, won. Worthy of note was the enthusiasm with which the players, many of them known pacifists, responded to the frenzy of the Game. Arden said later that he wished to demonstrate the ease with which emotions can be whipped-up by unprincipled demagogues. In failing to explain whether his demagogues were freedom-loving or totalitarian, however, Arden again lost on points in the objectivity stakes. The death-sentences on the losers, allotted by the time-honoured Roman thumbs-up-or-down symbolism, were carried out only in mime. Thus far Law and Order was disingenuously complied with: though it was open to doubt whether Theatre-of-Cruelty addict Margaretta D'Arcy would not have preferred to go further.

## Pornographic vengeance

Between bouts of this juvenile amusement (reminiscent more of freshman-hazing sessions in a cornbelt college than of New York's sophisticated comprehension of the complex issues involved in the for-real Vietnam tragedy) a series of improvised Interludes were presented before the breathless audience. The Ardens and their student dupes had constructed a 'play' in twenty four episodes, purporting to be an allegory of US involvement in S.E. Asia. Masked actors developed an incredible story of how a nuclear device is dropped by mistake on a lonely Appalachian valley by a USAF bomber (in tasteless reminiscence of the Palomares miscalculation, which none the less had gone far to convince patriot Caudillo Franco that we will stop at nothing to preserve the Spaniards from recrudescence of Red Rule). Affected by the fall-out from the explosion, a family of Tobacco Road Share-croppers begin to glow in the dark. In the belief that they had been smitten by the wrath of

God for playing cards on Sunday, they start a religious revival, to the disquiet of Administration elements who (naturally, according to the Arden–D'Arcy view of US credibility) are determined to hush-up the accident for keeps. Grandma, the aged matriarch of the family, is persuaded to run as Vice-President with LBJ in the next election, and implausibly gains office, only to find that her youngest son (played by student actor Pat McDermott, 22, balding would-be draft-dodger) is called upon to enlist to fight for freedom in Vietnam. In scenes of brutal caricature McDermott (aided by balding bearded-weirdy Leonardo Shapiro and other draft-abhorring NYU students) claims conscientous objector status, fails, carries his case to the Supreme Court and appeals on grounds that the war is unconstitutional.* Vice-President Grandma then unexpectedly impeaches LBJ upon the same cause and wins. But in a deft table-turning act she then announces her own (legal) declaration of war and personally escalates hostilities in a jet bomber over war-torn Vietnam. Her daughter Jezebel (now the President's daughter, for Grandma has moved swiftly into the White House upon the fall of LBJ – viciously MacBirded by actor Larry Pine) who has become a soldier's whore in Saigon – audience had had to wait long for sex-interest in Arden's show, but when it came it came with a pornographic vengeance – has been producing bombs instead of babies due to original nuclear fallout problems : and using Jezebel's womb in a scene of unrepeatable bestiality Grandma succeeds in blowing up all S.E. Asia.

## Subversive Adrian Mitchell

This curious saga was not the only dramatic offering of the day. The Ardens, taking strange liberties with regular professional dramatic conventions, had invited into the NYU theatre for free several outside groups and individual performers. These included

* So it is, not having been declared by Congress : but left-wing objections were not so marked in 1940 when FDR gave similarly unconstitutional aid to beleaguered Britain. Anarchist Arden's freedom to dissent was established for him in that year – he himself was then a nine-year-old.

the 'Bread and Puppet Theatre' (known for their blasphemous anti-war Christmas Crib established last year on steps of Cardinal Spellman's patriotic St Patrick's Cathedral), Joseph Chaikin's lyrics by British subversive Adrian Mitchell from anti-American subversive British show *US*, the girls' choir from the Bethel Baptist Church, Brooklyn (a clear attempt on the part of the Ardens to stir smouldering embers of last year's long hot summer – the Church has a Negro congregation), and noted Pekin dupe Conor Cruise O'Brien (sometime henchman of Red Black Kwame Nkrumah, as well as Butcher not only of the Congo but of CIA-backed *Encounter* magazine). There were also other participants whom space forbids to name: but the general tone was constant. Better Red than Dead as a Peacenik motto seemed transmuted to Better Red, Period: and this was to be borne out only too thoroughly in the anti-climatic climax of the whole performance.

## Sexual and sociological overtones

This arose out of the final episodes of the *Grandma* chronicle. Throughout the day the audience had been coming and going but a full hall had continued for approximately ten hours. When Grandma returned from her destruction of S.E. Asia it was to find that her C.O. son had raised a revolution in the United States and she and he, guided by the malevolent 'War-Gods' (who had paraded all day on their stilts, exhorting players and audience to acts and thoughts of violence) were forced to meet in a Freudian confrontation. Arden's (or was it D'Arcy's?) view of the American character seemed to involve a continuous tension between mother and son complete with sexual overtones. Grandma was by this time not only a mad old woman but also America – a kind of tabloid cartoon-style theatre that owed little to such naturalistic leftish writers of the thirties as Odets and Emile Zola. Sophisticated New York Critics found little of value in this wilful crudity, exacerbated as it was by the garish cardboard masks worn by the actors and the blatant delivery of their (improvised) dialogue straight into the 'lugholes'* of the audience. Thus revolution against the maternal parent

* Yorkshire-born Arden's habitual word for 'ears'.

meant revolution against Nation, and while actor McDermott rambled through a long diatribe on this subject, a Hungarian refugee (1956 vintage) called Paul Neuberg, who seemed to have forgotten what Krushchev's minions had done to his homeland, mounted the stage and commenced to sing a revolutionary song (drawn – he claimed – from the folklore of the Warsaw rising, and therefore presumably Red).* Within moments the audience was clapping and cheering in time to his minstrelsy. It was on the cards that a violent demonstration would have surged irresistibly out of the theatre into Second Avenue, thus provoking police action on an unprecedented scale – potential demonstrators numbered several score, if not one hundred: and New York's overworked cops might not have been able to bring more than 700-800 billy-club-toting lawmen to bear on the situation before it got completely out of hand, thus encouraging Ho Chi Minh to continue and even escalate his daily wanton bombing and napalm attacks upon Saigon. At this flashpoint of near-inevitable crisis, however, Arden dropped the mask.

## Free-sex double-think

Pushing his way among the frenzied actors (after nigh on 11 hours' performing they were still remarkably fresh – so fresh indeed that suspicions of narcotic-stimulation had already been aroused) Arden called a halt to further talk of revolution. 'Mr Nuremberg,' he said deliberately mispronouncing Neuberg's name for cheap dramatic effect, 'this is not a Nuremburg Rally.' He then went on to declare himself a CIA agent, charged with presenting theatre-of-dissent in order to see just how far dissent would go, and thus provide Washington watchdogs with a firm list of suspect students and NYU faculty-members. Shaken students and faculty-members, uncertain whether or no the British trouble-maker was telling the truth, fell into a sick silence. Arden's claim was plausible enough. His pay came from NYU funds: and NYU funds, like nearly every other

* In 1945 the Warsaw Poles reacted violently against German occupation, thus weakening German stand in face of Soviet military power.

cultural and educational fund in the USA naturally have been
swollen over recent years through secret government pipelines.
Why not? Presumably a free people is permitted to educate its
children to play an informed part in the national struggle against
Communist influence whether from Russia, China, Hanoi, London,
Paris or Havana. But the new generation of unwashed, free-sex,
double-thinking cowards will have none of this good old-time patriotic common sense: and Arden's surprising revelation touched them
on the raw.

## One of them wore no bra

It also touched on the raw their half-formed hopes of immediate
revolution. Unwilling to act without their renegade British leader
who seemed to have abandoned them at the crucial moment: and
unable to follow the D'Arcy line of spontaneous anarchist involvement, the assembled juveniles sat tight, confused and disappointed.
The rest of the performance was predictable enough. Grandma and
her son killed each other, the War-Gods had their panoply pulled
off their backs, revealing ordinary students underneath, and Arden
with some feebleness called for more undressing. The finale consisted of two girls, clad in nothing but bikinis and paper flags
(alleged to be the flags of all the nations, but significantly omitting
those of the Communist bloc. Arden's explanation, that they are
not on sale in New York toystores, would scarcely pass muster in
the Kremlin, flattering though it may be to our patriotic store-
keepers), who proceeded to launch into an anti-national strip-
tease. Their nubile bodies were painted all over in red, white and
blue, which did not succeed in concealing the fact that at least one
of them wore no bra. When the paper flags were all torn off, Arden
tore up two of them – both Union Jacks* – then blandly announced
that spectators would have noted one flag missing, Old Glory, no
less: and Arden then proceeded to unpin from the wall a copy of

* Flag desecration is not an offence in demoralised Britain. In New
York State, however, it carries a maximum penalty of a five-hundred
dollar fine. Hopeful legislators currently press for the increase of this to
life-imprisonment.

this sacred fabric (for which better men than he have frequently, if repetitively, died. He himself is quoted as saying 'No one but an idiot ever died for a *flag*. For what the flag symbolises, no doubt they have died; but what does it symbolise now?'). Quietly with no sense of strain or even awareness that he was committing an overt act of civil disobedience, Arden desecrated the flag. He walked across it. He said it was better to burn a flag (though he would not burn this one as it belonged to NYU!) than to burn flesh. A tasteless slide of what purported to be a Vietnamese child burned by US napalm – though experts have testified that US napalm does not burn, it liberates, and any burnt children have been burnt by the Viet-Cong – was projected at this point upon a screen behind him. Professor Hoffman was here observed to leave the theatre.

## Topless girl unpunished

With a few brief words asking people who did not want to kill to join the Army, and people who did not want a war not to pay any taxes, Arden brought the show to an end. What did it all mean? Was Arden really a CIA agent? If so, he was not a very efficient one, because throughout the eleven hours of his mammoth Carnival, many people gave vent to views on US policy which can only have inflamed public contempt for such figures as the President, General Westmoreland, and Cardinal Spellman. Character assassination on this scale is difficult to live down: yet we may assume that LBJ and his Administration would not falter even if the whole nation decided to oppose the war. We are fortunate in having leaders who, having put their hand to the plough, will not turn back: and there are not many nations of the free world who can say the same. But the significant fact that Arden's flag-desecration and bosombaring antics remain at the time of writing unprosecuted in the courts would suggest he has strong protectors, and if they are not the CIA, then who are they? A theory that the University authorities deliberately hushed-up the impact of the Carnival for fear of scandal (and loss of endowment subsidies) will not hold water. NYU's balding ex-Marine Corps President Hester has never failed before to assert his patriotic and real-estate-accumulating ideals against all opposition in the University, and it is unlikely that the exhibition of a topless girl-student would be allowed to go unpunished. Sources near the President state categorically that he did in fact carpet Hoffman and Dean Corrigan (who had taken a convenient weekend in the country over the date of the Carnival) on precisely that ground. Hoffman is reported to have claimed on behalf of his department that he observed no nipples on any young woman (true enough for the shifty nifty side-stepping Prof – mammary extremities were entirely overpainted red, white and blue). Taxed with his failure to prevent the flag-trampling, he quipped evasively: 'Sure, take a look at the goddam flag, why doncha? Say, we didn't even have ta send it to the dry-cleaners . . .' Such blatant equivocation will do little to further the feisty drama-coach's agit-property-conscious career: was this maybe Arden's ulterior intent, whether inspired by the Pentagon or the Kremlin? Neither establishment has any use for academic so-called 'freedom': and rightly so. For the Moscow moguls, freedom spells freedom, and therefore must be abolished absolutely. For our own Defence Department, it too often indicates undesirable subversion in the face of the common enemy, and is therefore under current investigation by the FBI.

To sum up: despite all the Ardens could do, the war in Vietnam continues. Only a day or two after their unpleasant pseudo-showbiz eructation, President Johnson put his Marines into the demilitarised zone. Soon, no doubt, he will put them into North Vietnam itself. Where will Arden be then? Where will be his fantastic so-called wife? Where will be his student claque?

As *Time* Magazine Editor-in-chief Hedley Donovan, a trustee of New York University, said to NYU's graduating class a few weeks back: 'The incredibly audacious thing that a few million people in South Vietnam and we Americans are trying to do is to defend not so much a nation as the possibility that South Vietnam can become a nation . . . You know, we might just succeed, and if that happens I hope that the many thoughtful dedicated Americans who oppose the policy will be glad to acknowledge that their country is sometimes capable of even more than we should dare to dream.'

# Some Notes from New York

## 1967

The first note from New York is actually a note from San Francisco.
A friend of mine was recently over there having a look at the
hippie-scene or whatever you care to call it in Haight-Ashbury.
There have been great fears expressed of a hippie explosion there
this summer as the drop-out generation converges from all points
east, full of love, dreams and banana scrapings. It all sounded
rather exhilarating, but the reality, I gather, is less so. My friend
compared Haight-Ashbury to a refugee camp: San Francisco, although on the Pacific coast, can be remarkably cold, and many of the
hippies who arrive are not at all prepared for the rigours of fending
for themselves in a sympathetic but basically unorganised community. Many are very young with children and there is something
of a health problem.

The group known as the Diggers tries to ameliorate conditions:
they are a politically committed group who are to some extent based
on the English seventeenth-century agrarian revolutionaries, and
they have some farms in California. They also distribute food in
San Francisco, and (I believe) clothing. But they are a little non-
plussed by the attitude of many of the hippies who have not entirely rid themselves of their American middle-class mores, and
who expect to find 'leaders' in Haight-Ashbury. Leaders, to the
Diggers, are a non-existent concept.

Clearly there is a great possibility of a real mess there if the
overcrowding continues. Rumours, well-substantiated, suggest that

certain evil-minded elements in the city are endeavouring to make trouble between the hippies and the Negroes, so that if there are race-riots this summer (as well there might be) the hippies will bear the brunt thereof and this will serve as a pretext to run them out of town. America is, in part, now being run as though it were a British or Roman Imperial province – *divide et impera*, et cetera. The love-generation may soon take on the tragic aspect of the Children's Crusade in the eleventh century. But if the Diggers' hard-headed anarchistic philosophy prevails, such a fate could be averted.

Another phenomenon reminiscent of the Roman Empire was the great 'Support our boys in Vietnam' parade in New York on 13 May. There was no Caesar leading the parade in his chariot (and indeed nothing much to 'triumph' over anyway) but Cardinal Spellman was on the saluting base as the flag-waving, boozing marchers swaggered past. The peace parade a month earlier had marched in peace and the only incidents were some eggs and rude words shouted at the demonstrators by spectators. The war parade marched offensively, and the only incidents were attacks by marchers upon spectators. A long-haired youth was tarred and feathered, some girls and boys who tried to enter the parade (as supporters of *soldiers* – soldiers being human beings – but not of the war) were beaten and had paint poured on them. Drunken hooligans flooded the town later in the evening. A huge thug, drunk, with a bottle in one hand and a flag in the other, was seen to lurch into a Second Avenue theatrical (off-off Broadway theatrical) bar and stand around in a menacing attitude, defying the arty clientele to desecrate his flag. I don't think anyone did. He was apparently a *very* huge thug.

Another difference between the war and the peace marches was that the peace marchers assembled individually: the war marchers were largely made up from organised groups, the American Legion, the *police*, school children, right-wing trade unionists. The latter seem to have supplied themselves with unlimited quantities of beer to keep their spirits up (in case they were attacked by drug-maddened peaceniks, no doubt), and it was from these groups that the tar and feathers were also available. They are not normally available on Fifth Avenue on a Saturday afternoon.

A strange conversation in a Greenwich Village newsagent the other day. A very beautiful working-class girl with an un-reproducible American-Jewish accent asked the (Jewish) shopkeeper for a sheet of notepaper and an envelope. She wished to write a letter to a Rabbi – so the paper must be of good quality – did the shopman want to know her name – it was the same name as that of a very famous Rabbi who led thousands of Jews out of Spain in the days of the Inquisition – the shopman hadn't heard of him, huh? So the shopman don't know his Jewish History so good. So he thought of nothing all the time but making more money, money, money – why wasn't he in the synagogue all day and *pray*? Pray for what? Pray for Israel, what else – 'Don't you read your newspapers? You have children? Sure you have children. So why don't you send them to Israel? So why don't you send them to Israel, let them fight for their people – money, money, money – I think it's just disgusting !' Then she fixed me with a look as I waited in the queue behind her. I quailed. It was as though the prophetess Deborah was risen again. I rather hope she isn't. Such people, like Shaw's Saint Joan, are splendid to look back upon, but uncomfortable to have around. There are altogether too many uncomfortable people around just at present.

# A First Class Texas Job

## 1966

*Review of:*
Rush to Judgement, by Mark Lane (Bodley Head). Inquest,
by E. J. Epstein (Hutchinson).

Somebody once said that 'the man on the Clapham omnibus' was
the sort of typical figure of average common sense whom judges,
juries, lawyers and the like ought to have at the back of their minds
as a point of reference when considering complex and over-technical
legal problems. If this anonymous traveller does not have the expert knowledge and confidential sources of information possessed
by the police or the pathologists or the psychiatrists, at least, so runs
the argument, he may have some degree of intelligent objectivity
that can enable him to distinguish wood from trees and thus come
a little nearer to a just understanding of the truth. He seems to have
been referred to very infrequently during the inquiries concerning
the death of President Kennedy on 22 November 1963.

Now I myself do not often travel to Clapham, and I have not
personally consulted 'the man on the omnibus'. The nearest I got
to him was perhaps 'the man at the Dublin dinner party', the evening of the day upon which it was announced that Oswald had been
shot by Ruby. The conversation turned naturally upon the news
from Dallas; indeed, it did more than turn, it was obsessed by it.
'Who do you think did it?' 'What's your interpretation?' 'Is any of
the official story likely to be true?' et cetera. Then this man said:

'Whoever did it, and for whatever reason, there is no doubt in
my mind that the whole thing is a first class Texas job.'

I asked him exactly what he meant and he replied, in effect:

'You go to the cinema, don't you? You enjoy Western films? Well, Dallas is a great modern city, as far as its material way of life is concerned; but spiritually it is still more or less a wide-open cow town of the 1880s, and the murders of Kennedy and Oswald and Tippit belong to that period of history. Whatever their subsequent effects upon the history of our own time, they must be viewed through the appropriate retrospective lenses, which in this case are the lenses of a film camera. It doesn't have to be a good film, even. The Wild West in its own time saw itself as a mythological age and dramatised itself in exactly the same way as the cinema has done ever since.'

Let me give one example of this self-dramatisation which I found out about later: a civilian motorist in Texas is apparently permitted, by state law, to carry a gun in his map compartment on the grounds that 'saddle holsters' are a necessary provision for self defence when making a journey across the desert; nobody knows when rustlers, Mexican bandits, Injuns or Billy the Kid might not suddenly turn up.

And turn up they did, with a vengeance, in Dallas, in 1963.

So let me, being a dramatist by trade and not a lawyer like Mr Lane nor an academic like Mr Epstein, set out a few notions for a film sequence of just such a 'first class Texas job'. We are in Texas, around 1880, and an important person, much loved and much hated, is about to arrive in town. He does not have to be the President; he need be no more than the fearless, hard-hitting editor of a newspaper who has been exposing a number of local financial scandals involving large scale cattle transactions and various dubious deals with the Apaches. He is believed to be interested in examining the causes of a recent and nearly disastrous Indian rising, and he is known to be anxious to find ways and means of coming to some sort of accommodation with, say, Geronimo, the scourge of the south-west. He has expressed the opinion that the said scourge has been unduly provoked by the US Cavalry in alliance with the Texas

Rangers and, more important, he is being listened to in Washington. He is played by Spencer Tracy.

As the stage coach swings into the dung-covered main street, a volley of shots rings out and Mr Tracy falls back into his seat, dead. Confusion in the street. Everyone runs backwards and forwards and guns go off all round the compass. From the Sheriff's Office emerges the Sheriff (Dean Jagger) yelling, 'Some renegade's shot the Editor !' The cry is taken up from end to end of the town, and after having utilised about thirty seconds of sound track it becomes, rather strangely, metamorphosed into a shout of 'That half-breed's shot the Editor !' Immediate rush of persons to a shack on the edge of the desert in which dwells Anthony Perkins, half-breed and generally disreputable character. When the posse, or lynch mob, or whatever it is, gets to the shack, it is to discover Mr Perkins standing, bewildered, over the corpse of the Sheriff's Deputy (Lee Marvin). A smoking gun lies beside the porch, and the half-breed's redskin wife (Jean Simmons) grovels in the dust, screaming hysterically. Perkins is hauled off to jail, and the Sheriff, his thumb in his waistcoat, a shotgun in the crook of his elbow, and an ambiguous smile under his moustache, makes a great performance of telling everyone within earshot that:

'This man's gonna git a fair trial or else Ah wanta know the reason why. An' he's gonna git his fair trial at ten o'clock on Tuesday mornin', and at precisely ten o'clock on Tuesday mornin' Ah'm abringin' him out o' this yar jail house and Ah'm atakin' him across the street to that thar court house and no one's agoin' to stop me !'

Short interlude inside the jail during which Mr Perkins rattles the bars and shrieks: 'You can't hang an innocent man !' And then, Tuesday morning. Amidst a roaring, muttering, definitely overacting crowd of unwashed extras, the prisoner is led out of the jail. A pause on the veranda while the Sheriff addresses a few more self-congratulatory remarks to the citizens. Then, suddenly, through the press comes Frank Sinatra (or perhaps Dean Martin) in a character part: a beat-up gambler who has been established as alternately beating up and making love to the girls in the saloon. He has also been established as a great pal of Mr Jagger and also of Mr Marvin, and with a swift lunge of his right arm he fires six successive bullets straight into Mr Perkins' stomach.

He then breaks down and sobs out something about 'That Editor was a fine man and he had the sweetest little wife this side of the Rio Grande. She never knew I existed even, but I'm telling you all, I did it for her sake'. Further up the street, a slow track of the camera reveals a group of well-fed gentlemen in frock coats and spotless Stetsons, smoking cheroots and apparently very much at ease with the world. They are on the steps of the Inter-State Cattlemen's Bank and Trading Assoc Inc, and among their frock coats is at least one blue and braided cavalry uniform.

Now any ordinary audience will have a very fair idea of what such a sequence means. It means that a reel or two later James Stewart is going to discover on behalf of the 'simple, decent people of this state' (i.e. a group of hymn-singing smallholders, at feud with the cattlemen, and suspicious of Mr Stewart, because he is supposed to be a professional gunfighter) that the Sheriff, the Deputy, and a number of others are all in a conspiracy, backed by the frock coats and the uniform, to kill Mr Tracy and implicate Mr Perkins (who, being a half-breed, has no friends). The actual shots at the stage coach were probably fired by Mr Marvin, though Mr Perkins may have been blackmailed into expending at least one cartridge, and Mr Marvin, unfortunately, has made a mess of his second assignment, which was to kill Mr Perkins before he could be arrested, so the Sinatra/Martin character has had to be called in to finish the job. This was unwise, because being such an unstable individual, he is liable to overdo it. His fervent expressions of devotion to the Editor's wife are an example of his injudicious zeal in this direction.

Of course, the flaw in this argument is fairly obvious. Had the Sheriff been played by John Wayne rather than Dean Jagger, the audience would take an entirely different interpretation, and there would be no need to put James Stewart under contract at all, because Mr Wayne would clearly be able to wind up the story on his own, positively oozing independent integrity. But in fact, in Dallas, three years ago, there was no John Wayne, and a great deal of trouble was taken to see that there was to be no James Stewart either. Nevertheless, after one or two false claimants (terrible old hams, for the most part, whose mouthings and sawings of the air would convince very few Clapham commuters) he has turned up. He is, of course, Mark Lane, and he has been given some unexpected and not entirely sympathetic assistance by Edward Jay Epstein.

Mr Lane comes into the business as the legal adviser of Mrs Oswald, mother of the alleged assassin, and he attended (or rather, tried to attend, for there was great resentment against him, and he was pretty successfully obstructed) the meetings of the Warren Commission in order to guard the posthumous interests of her unhappy son. As Oswald was dead there was no regular trial for murder. The Warren Commission was supposed to find out who had done the murder: but in fact, as Mr Lane clearly establishes in his book, they began their sessions with an unconscious (one could almost say conscious) assumption that the Dallas police and the FBI were quite right and that the arrested man was in fact the guilty man. Thus the evidence brought forward into the Commission's final summary of its report is nearly all what one would call 'prosecution evidence'. Other ('defence') evidence was heard by the Commission, and it appears in the supplementary volumes of the report (all twenty-six of them). Mr Lane has collated this raw material with the Commission's own summing up and interpretation of it in the first volume; and he has come to the conclusion, from which it is difficult to dissent, that a jury at Oswald's trial (had he been alive to have faced one) might very well have brought in a verdict of 'not guilty', if only because there was insufficient weight of proof presented.

The witnesses before the Warren Commission were not cross-examined in the interests of the accused, and a great many inconsistencies, contradictions, evasions and downright lies were allowed to go unquestioned, the Commission being anxious to show that

Oswald and nobody else killed Kennedy, that Oswald and nobody else killed Tippit, and that Ruby killed Oswald without assistance, encouragement, inducement or even motive. Ruby, you see, like Oswald, was barmy; therefore the consistency of his acts need not be examined, he could not have been part of a conspiracy, and America (implies the Commission) can turn over and go to sleep again untroubled. Such, in brief, is Mark Lane's thesis.

And such is also the general tenor of Mr Epstein's book. This work is not, in origin, a partisan piece of writing. It is based indeed, upon an objective survey of the actual workings of the Commission itself, and those members who provided the author with his information must by now be feeling a little queasy. But Earl Warren, it has been argued, is an excellent famous Judge, whose services to the cause of right and liberal truth have been innumerable. His fellow commissioners were men of proven integrity; indeed, great care was taken to exclude 'controversial' figures from the Commission, whatever that means, but we have Mr Epstein's word that it was done.

Can we then believe that such an honourable assembly could sit down to examine a notorious and outrageous crime and then calmly agree to hush it up and paper it over? At this point Mr Epstein gets nervous. He points out, rightly, that in fact the Commission was not quite all it appeared to be. The senior members did not sit continuously; some of them hardly attended at all. But then they were busy public servants and had other responsibilities. So much of the detailed work of taking and evaluating evidence was left to their junior assistants. These, in turn, relied upon the FBI and other investigatory bodies for the greater part of their work, and if a group of young and ambitious lawyers should be a little embarrassed and more than a little deferential in the face of *ex cathedra* pronouncements from the mighty J. Edgar Hoover, FBI chief, then we should be neither surprised nor condemnatory. There may have been inefficiency, there was certainly undue haste, but there was no villainous collusion. Besides, anyone can make a mistake; and the interests of public order were well served. The Commission, it may be claimed, is vindicated by its results: Oswald was found to have done everything he was supposed to have done, and nothing else; and there were no race riots, insurrections or further assassinations.

No, that is not quite true. If we refer to Mr Lane at this point, we discover that afterwards, in Dallas, there were one or two mysterious deaths and assaults and outbreaks of threat. Of course, Dallas is Dallas, where map compartments in a motor car are saddle holsters on a horse, and it might happen to anyone down there. But why did it have to happen to Mr Lane's particular list of people, who had all offered evidence that in some way might have helped, had it been examined more closely, to clear Oswald of guilt, or at least to provide him with one or more confederates?

So perhaps there was a conspiracy? My own view is that there certainly was. But it need not have been a very big one. We do not have to indulge ourselves with the seductive myths of international plots, which is a game leading rapidly to McCarthyite hysteria and theories about the 'Protocols of Zion'. But suppose there were a few men in Dallas who hated Kennedy (John Birchers or petty racialists seem the most plausible suggestions) who were also in a position to cover their tracks with the assistance of *some* of the local police? For instance, when Oswald was brought out to the car that was to take him to the prison, there was a tremendous guard of lawmen to protect him in the fatal basement; but at the crucial moment, there was no car in position. So they all had to stand and wait for the vehicle, with their prisoner well to the fore, not even covered by a blanket in the time-honoured British way; and when Ruby came forward he found Oswald so liberally presented to his gun that he might have been put there on purpose. Perhaps he was. Anyway, the local police had some awkward questions to face. The FBI did not make them any more awkward than they had to. Why not? Well, there is a question that Oswald might have been an FBI agent. The mighty Hoover, beating as he swept as he cleaned, flatly said that this was not the case. The Commission took his word and thanked him fulsomely for his co-operation.

Does this mean that the whole thing was an FBI job? I do not think so. Even if a presumably sophisticated man like Hoover believed that Kennedy alone was responsible for the conception and working-out of policies unsatisfactory by FBI standards (which would no doubt, to Hoover, have meant treasonable policies), it is not inevitable that such policies would be reversed by killing Kennedy. It is much more likely that the FBI is as the Church of Rome or the Communist Party and cannot bear to admit error. Therefore a rumour that his smallest of small-fry informants was mixed up in the death of the President would appear to the mighty Hoover like an arrow in the heel to the godlike Achilles, and it would have to be prevented by whatever means came first to hand. If such a means was the murder of Oswald then it would have to be done. It would be organised by some dedicated servant of the public good, carried out by a convenient near-criminal (Ruby), and covered up by the blandest of Olympian denials. Such events take place daily in the world of the secret police, and the public enjoys them weekly in the world of the cinema, but it is rare that their repercussions interest quite so many people in quite so many places as happened on this particular occasion.

The apparently pusillanimous reaction of the Warren Commission need not upset us too much – unless, of course, we are the sort of people who really do believe that an honest man in public life has only to be honest and all falsehood will flee before him. Imagine yourself to be Earl Warren or one of his colleagues confronted by a piece of evidence suggesting that Oswald was involved with the FBI, and that the FBI are covering this up. Or that Oswald's hiding-place in the book-depository was not the only place from which shots were fired at the presidential motorcade. Or that Ruby and Tippit and a well-known rightist called Weissman had a meeting in Ruby's stripclub a whole week before the murders. (All these suggestions were in fact made, and were rejected by the Commission on not very adequate grounds.) Now, what are you going to do? You have three choices:

1. Hush the whole thing up, silence the inconvenient witnesses by trumped-up charges of drug-addiction and whatnot, and publish

nothing at all of the truth.

2. Accept the 'Oswald defence' evidence as at least as plausible as the rest (which it was, as Mr Lane makes clear).

3. Publish all the evidence, but contrive to denigrate those parts of it that do not fit the preconceived theory.

The true dishonest conspirator would follow course number 1. This is what was apparently done by the Dallas police and perhaps by the FBI. But the Commissioners did not. Nor did they follow course number 2. If they had, they would really have been in trouble. They might have had to find that Oswald was innocent, in which case who was guilty? Or that he had associates, and then who would they be? Heaven knows what would turn up. Why, LBJ is a Texan. Suppose some friends of his were mixed up in it? Even if he cleared himself, to the satisfaction of the Commission, what would the public think? Let alone the Republicans. And who among the loyal Commission (appointed by the President) would dare to ask the President to clear himself? Lord Denning's little job was cushy compared with this. The nation, as they say, would be plunged into anarchy. The most liberal of judges would surely blench at such a prospect.

So we are left with course number 3. They did indeed publish nearly all of what they were told. But they did not enlarge upon it, when it posed too many questions, and they published it in no fewer than twenty-six volumes. You need stamina to read them all and separate wheat from chaff, and there was plenty of chaff. To assist the weary student and to prepare the newspapers of the world, the Commission's conclusions, tendentious and half baked, were carefully listed in the first volume and only a man with a direct interest in the case, like Mark Lane, would trouble to read further, *and make notes as he read*.

Which brings us to a final point. Anyone, a year or two ago, who ventured to suggest that Mark Lane might have some pertinent things to say, and should be encouraged to say them, was subjected to an extraordinary campaign of vilification from quite unexpected directions: *The Guardian*, where a Mr Grigg threw such words as 'renegade' (see my improvised film treatment above!), *The New Statesman*, and even *Peace News*, they all came swinging in about our heads, demanding resignations, retractions and general public breast beating. But now Mr Lane has written his book. He may not be right; he is, after all, no more than an advocate. But as an advocate he presents the side of the case that no one wanted to hear. The Warren Commission desired above all to preserve public order and a quiet mind in time of trouble. Agreeable objects, but if we possess them at the expense of the truth, we are not likely to be able to enjoy them for very long.

# Not All That Representative

## 1968

*Review of:*
The New Legions, by Donald Duncan (Gollancz).

I was sent this book for review several months ago and the features
editor of *Peace News* has lately been dropping polite but unmis-
takable hints that if I don't intend to write anything about it I had
better hand it over to a more energetic commentator pretty sharpish.
I have responded with excuses of ill-health and pressure of work, all
true but not really adequate: and now that I have at last forced
myself to the typewriter I am puzzled to account for my procrastina-
tion. For some reason I have clearly not wanted to read and discuss
this quite straightforward volume. Why?

Let me summarise the contents briefly. Mr Duncan, having been
discharged ('honourably' and well-decorated) from the US Army
Special Forces (the 'Green Berets') has written an account of his
voluntary recruitment therein, his training for counter-insurgency
operations, his service in Vietnam, and his final revulsion against
the work he had to do and the military system that imposed its
values on him for many years of his life. He is now military editor
of the radical magazine *Ramparts* and a well-known speaker at
anti-war rallies in the States, where he provides a useful counter to
the argument that opposition to the American policy comes primarily from unrepresentative hippies and traitorous reds.

He is of course not all that representative himself: the number of
Master-Sergeants with the US Silver Star and the Legion of Merit
who are so convinced that all their labour has been in vain that they
will stand on public platforms to say so, and who are at the same

time literate enough to make their declaration coherently in print, is never likely to be very large. Nevertheless, Mr Duncan exists, and it is good that he does.

So what has been upsetting me? The book begins with a chapter describing the author's induction into the Army several years ago, when Vietnam was still a problem for the French and when the maps most often pored over on the Pentagon tables were those of Central Europe. The scenes at the medical examination of the draftees (Mr Duncan began as a conscript and only signed on as a regular some time later) are vividly described: and apart from little local peculiarities, such as the *communal* inspection of anal areas and the oath-taking ritual, they do not differ very much from those in which I myself participated in a back room of some untenanted shops in Sheffield in 1949 when I was formally acknowledged as one of King George's men.

I did not think very much about the implications of military service at that time (neither, of course, did Mr Duncan) and though our respective tours of duty had little in common (I spent eighteen inglorious months idling in an Edinburgh office and going to the pictures) we were both part of the same outrageous system and it took both of us a very long time to come to realise just how outrageous that system is.

I suppose it is silly to be so worried today about not having been a conscientious objector eighteen years ago *in peacetime* that I found myself physically unable to take a book like Mr Duncan's in my hand and study it: but there it is: I have had to look back on my own life and set it out in comparison with those of many young men in America at this moment, and I realise that I can offer them very little by way of precept or example.

Incidentally, *The New Legions* might well prove equally uncomfortable reading even for those who *did* declare themselves as C.O.s. Duncan says:

'Rather than go to jail, young men docilely register for the draft, even though it violates their consciences, and then are "given" the option to apply as conscientious objectors. By allowing the military to rule their consciences, they forfeit to it the right to define conscience and morality. By registering and then applying for C.O. status, the individual is saying "The system is okay, but make *him* a killer, not me." A person conscientiously opposed to killing should not have to cooperate with a system designed to promote it.'

This is a nasty argument: but in view of the author's horrifying analysis of the contemporary American war machine and how it came into being since 1945, it is difficult to reject it.

America is in fact a community geared to war quite as much as was ever Sparta in the fifth century BC or Prussia in the eighteenth century AD: and it is only the fag-end of an earlier tradition still lingering in the mouths of school-teachers and lawyers and politicians that prevents the majority of the population from realising it. A nice man I met in New York last year, who had served in the Korean War and told many funny stories about it, remarked on the absence of *moustaches* on the faces of GIs today. Who had decided that they should no longer be worn, he wondered, and for what reason? Was it not true, he asked me, that in the 1940s the American soldiers were laughed at by their British comrades for the sloppiness of their turnout and the length of their hair? Yes, indeed it was, and I have an old volume of Giles cartoons from immediately after World War II to confirm this. Did I not think, he continued, that there was something not altogether wrong with an Army about which such jokes could be made, and was it not sinister that this was no longer the case?

There is a whole world of difference between Master-Sergeant Duncan being carefully taught *not* to torture prisoners (with a discursive description of the forbidden torments added by the instructor, significantly *gratis*) and General Washington's buck-skinned levies mustering nervously in front of the local court-houses, muskets in their hands and fear of the redcoats barely overcome in their stomachs. If the majority of Americans have as much private difficulty in reading this book as I had, it is a difference that may very well be understood too late.

Nevertheless, Mr Duncan exists: and he has opened his own eyes. It is not at all impossible that sufficient of the others will let him open theirs.

# A Remonstration about Rhodesia

## 1969

I am sorry I did not write the report that John Ball was hoping for about the occcupation by a group of writers of Rhodesia House on the Tuesday before the Sunday of the big demonstration there. There was in fact remarkably little to report.

We got in at 10.30 am by pretending to be *bona fide* visitors, we got put out firmly but 'correctly' by the constabulary at 3 pm; and in the meantime we had sat around and stood around and not noticeably obstructed the operation of the building. The flag remained illegally flying on its pole, such business as had to be transacted at the counter was transacted by the staff (they were crowded by us into a corner, but they were ladies, and could hardly be ejected) and some posters were put up in the windows announcing that the building was now in the hands of the 'people of Zimbabwe' – which, except for one cheerful African who arrived at lunchtime, seemed far from the truth.

The lavatories were closed off to us. Some Fascists came and put up their poster – they were such a significant peer-group of Mr Smith's that it seemed better to leave them be, after a little argument. (They were also large and determined-looking.) A group of LSE students who came to reinforce us later in the day were, I think, a little put out by the amateurish nature of the whole affair. They were certainly most patronising. But what else could they expect from a miscellaneous group of literary gents and ladies?

Without about 500 militant students it would not have been possible to get any further in the building, and without about 5,000 militant students and workers it would not have been possible to have stayed there for any appreciable length of time. In order to get such help, we would have had to advertise our intentions rather widely beforehand, and someone might have been forewarned. A groups of writers acting in concert can normally do little more than sign a communal letter to *The Times*. Even then they are always held up by some stylistic individualist who wants the whole thing re-written before he will sign it.

There was no literary significance about crowding out the foyer of a public building, so therefore no overt mutual acrimony among us: but equally no great political dynamism. It was quiet and liberal and polite and exactly the sort of thing for which I recently (and unfairly) suggested William Morris might be gently mocked.

Exactly where one finds a really workable, politically-valuable mode of civil disobedience between the two extremes (our sort of thing, on the one hand, and the following Sunday's pushing and shoving and bashing, on the other) I really do not know. If you are quiet and polite, and small in numbers, you can probably get in anywhere (*for a very short time*): if you are loud and rough, and come in crowds, you probably can't (at least not without your crowd being large enough and varied enough to be something like a cross-section of the population, or not without the kind of violence that they have recently been having in Tokyo: and clearly not enough of us are ready for *that*: yet).

I am not ashamed of having taken part: but I am not exultant either. A pinprick of embarrassment was obviously caused – for why did the Law wait until 3 pm to throw us out, and then announce beforehand that there would be no arrests? A difficult question for the Government to answer had been posed in dramatic form. But the style of theatre was more like the old West End with teacups*

* *Footnote (1976):*
We did not in fact drink tea. Mr Ronald Segal (the writer who set the whole thing going, and is, I believe, from Rhodesia – thus making the 'people of Zimbabwe' up to at least the number of two, contrary to

than anything *avant-garde*. With temperatures all over the globe at the height they are, does such old-world behaviour act as a much-needed corrective, or is it merely futile?

I do not believe there is a right answer to that. You reply according to your temperament and taste, not according to your wisdom or to some fundamental truth. People's temperaments and tastes vary a great deal from one day to the next, according to all sorts of circumstances.

There are days when I despise genteel and gradual liberals: there are days when I thank God for them. Consistent and logical attitudes are splendid things to have around, until they come into headlong conflict. Yet your flexible man, who will adjust himself with care to each coming situation, too often ends up like Harold Wilson, making *all* the wrong choices from something like the best of motives.

What an unreliable set of creatures we are, to be sure. In the words of Adrian Mitchell, it's enough to make a man 'piss off and write a poem about ants'.

---

what I wrote above) had been at school with the Rhodesia House official who confronted us. An attempt therefore was made to cool the affair down by means of the old boy network ... 'Why, Ronnie, it's not *you*! Look here, why don't you all have a cup of tea while you're waiting for the police ...?' But we did not drink tea. Despite our liberalism, we were not seduced. We did not address Mr Segal's sometime school-fellow as a Fascist Swine: but we refused his cups of tea. I think it important to commemorate such little victories over one's own instinctively accommodating sloppiness ...

# Part Three

# The Matter of Ireland

My artistic and political development in the years following the trip to America is fairly enough summarised in the essays which follow. The work I have done with D'Arcy in Ireland (or rather, some of it, because our play *The Ballygombeen Bequest* is subject to litigation and cannot at present be written about – which makes for a deep lacuna in the account of the genesis of *The Non-Stop Connolly Show*) will be seen to have been much more closely connected with the practical politics of parties and doctrines than anything heretofore. Our joint experience in India, 1969–70, of course has a good deal to do with this: but it really began earlier.

In 1968 many things had come to a head. There was the revolt of the students and workers in France, with all the consequent excitement exported abroad from it. There was the frenzy of police brutality at the Chicago Democratic Convention. There was the Russian invasion of Czechoslovakia. There was the massacre in Mexico at the time of the Olympic Games. There was the prohibition by Stormont Unionism of a perfectly reasonable Civil Rights March in Derry, the incorrect accusation that Northern Irish Civil Rights was a front for the IRA, the savage attack upon the marchers who had the nerve to defy the ban, and the inexorable slide of the largely-forgotten Irish problem into the maelstrom of blood and bitterness which to this day swirls wider and wider.

On a personal level, there was an attempt by D'Arcy and myself to work for the first time in collaboration with an overtly Socialist group of actor-playwrights (CAST) – at the overtly Socialist Unity Theatre. *Harold Muggins was a Martyr*, the play which all together we jointly created\*, was perhaps no great shakes – certainly the

* see page 46

critics seemed to have small idea what it was we were up to – but
the occasion of its presentation did give rise to a remarkable conference, rally, symposium of many left-wing artistic groups and individuals who, maybe for the first time, were made aware of each
other and their respective work: and who were enabled in many
cases to establish joint action and permanent cultural/political contacts.

There was the production of *The Hero Rises Up* at the Institute
of Contemporary Arts, when D'Arcy and myself discovered the
limitations of such bodies as the midwives of free experiment.
Libertarianism – if it trod too far out of line – could be chopped off
at the neck by those whose public postures had always been so
erect in its defence. We quarrelled with the ICA on specific professional issues: our right as co-author-directors to compose our own
publicity material, our right to manage the production the way we
wanted it managed, and our right to determine the type of audience
we thought would be best served by the show we were putting on.
In isolation the argument could be regarded as ephemeral and un-
important. But taken in conjunction with the general mood and
events of the time it seemed an ill augury. We were genuinely –
if naïvely – flabbergasted by the sudden and fearful rigidity of the
ICA officials: had the day at last arrived when gentlemanly accommodation of artistic and administrative differences in the theatre
would be no longer possible? And, if so, what did this bode for our
work in the future?

Straws in the wind in the 'Year of the Pig' ... and by no means
alone: the detective at Holyhead and the lady from Brixton
Prison were also well aware that things were closing in ... Conor
Cruise O'Brien, as holder of the Albert Schweitzer Chair of
political and literary studies at NYU, had been a genial and liberal
man to work under in that university, exuding a healthy scepticism
of all men of affairs and their alleged *bona fides*. By 1969 he had
entered formal party-politics in his own country: and at the time
of writing he is Minister for Posts and Telegraphs in the Dublin
Coalition Government. As such he is responsible for the censorship
of all material put over radio or television which in any way may be
deemed to assist the cause of 'subversive elements'. He has left the
Irish in no doubt that when the tocsin sounds he can be every bit
as rigorous as Mayor Daley or Mr Brezhnev.

# The Third World seen from the First

## 1972

*Review of:*
Murderous Angels, a play by Conor Cruise O'Brien
(Hutchinson).

When Dr Cruise O'Brien stood for the Irish Parliament in the Labour interest two years ago, he was quoted as saying that Ireland ought to be considered as a part of the Third World. This remark was not well-received by the Dublin political establishment; and although it did not lose him votes in his metropolitan constituency, it does not seem to have done his party much good in the rural areas, where the 'Third World', if thought about at all, suggests primarily the collection-boxes for foreign missions on every grocery counter which bear a picture of a little black baby appealing mutely for Catholic Salvation. His own views, under stress of the Ulster crisis, appear since to have suffered something of a change and he is now accused of seeking to creep closer to England than is thought patriotic in an Irish legislator. I don't want to become involved in the current Irish game of Cruise O'Brien-baiting, which is largely the prerogative of the right-wing (Provisional) IRA and their big-business associates, though the quarry has given as good as he gets – but the circumstance has some relevance to the treatment of the character of Lumumba in this play about the Congo tragedy.

Dr Cruise O'Brien was ideally equipped to write upon the subject – he worked in the Congo for the UNO, he knew Hammarskjöld, he knew Tshombe and Tshombe's men who murdered Lumumba, he understood the role played by the great powers and by the western financial interests, and (although himself a white man), he was, as an Irishman, sufficiently untainted by imperialism to be accepted and perhaps even trusted by Africans. Yet when *Murderous Angels* was produced last year in Paris by Joan Little-wood, we read in the press that the author was made unhappy by a serious disagreement over the interpretation of Lumumba. The black actors in the cast, it seems, insisted on Miss Littlewood presenting the character in an unrealistic and idealised manner, cutting out the eccentricities and disorderly behaviour which Dr Cruise O'Brien had carefully written for the part. Lumumba was a racial hero: he must not be made ridiculous. There seem to have been no complaints about Hammarskjöld, who is shown in the play as being 'queer' in every sense of the word, and by no means the straightforward 'honest broker' that we took him for in his life-time.

I think the actors were right, and the author, judged entirely on his script, wrong. He has not succeeded in making Lumumba speak through his own mouth. He has had several subordinate characters speak a great deal about the ideals and intentions of the African leader: but Lumumba, when we see him – and it is only twice at any length – is shown drinking and laughing and cursing and making love, or else sunk into a fey resignation immediately before his death. Hammarskjöld, on the other hand, gets a well-rounded portrayal and is shown always immersed in the planning, explication and execution of his political affairs. We do not see him 'at home' or 'in his shirt-sleeves'. In fact, the two main person-ages of the play do not balance, and the dramatic structure demands they must, as Elizabeth and Mary Stuart are made to balance by Schiller, or Richard II and Bolingbroke, or Othello and Iago.

Despite Dr Cruise O'Brien's electoral platform, he is not really a man of the Third World. He is very much a man of the Western Bloc which destroyed Lumumba – a dissident member, certainly: and he analyses the moral weakness, the villainy, and the physical power of that bloc with great accuracy. But his is without doubt a play about Westerners, for Westerners. Judged by those standards, it is a very good play indeed – the National Theatre must be eternally despised for being too frightened to put it on – but it is the play of an author who finds himself talking to Harold Wilson when a solution to Irish problems is needed. I don't say Harold Wilson ought not to be talked to; if Dr Cruise O'Brien had gone to discuss Ulster with Castro, who in Dublin would ever have voted for him again? But I suspect that Dr Cruise O'Brien is much nearer his own Hammarskjöld than he was ready to believe when he set about writing his script.

# Politics and Prisons

## 1968

I have lately been involved with some work at Unity Theatre. This little play-house, founded in the days of socialist and anti-fascist enthusiasm before World War II, has (it is not unfair to say) fallen on evil days – for reasons I have not space to go into here – and has for some time seemed just another amateur theatre club, playing at erratic weekends to uncertain audiences.

The original political commitment of its founders, however, has not disappeared: though as an artistic force on the Left it has inevitably been somewhat muted. There was a time, during the McCarthy period, when a prosecution of Unity for a breach of the club-theatre regulations was plausibly interpreted as an attempt on the part of 'The Authorities' to muzzle an anti-American play that was then being staged. It is, however, unlikely that the theatre at present bulks very large in the card-index of that Special Branch or MI5 (or of whatever other agency is responsible for putting the boot into the crotches of our dissident artists).

But the other night a lady, well-known to me, who is employed as a psychiatrist on the staff of one of the London gaols, came to see our production. She came as an invited guest on a complimentary ticket. Afterwards she said to me that she would like to come again and bring some friends to see the show and, as she was not a member, how could she get tickets? Since Unity is in need of as many paying customers as it can get, I did not offer to have her complimentary ticket renewed, but suggested that she should join the Theatre Club (at a very modest charge, which she was certainly able to afford) and then she could come as often as she wished. To which she replied, in all seriousness, that she did not think she could become a member of Unity, because if it got known in the Prison Service that she was associated with such an organisation her job might be in jeopardy.

Now I must emphasise that this lady is no fool: it is quite clear from her conversation that within the confines of the prison where she works she will take a liberal and decent view of the men she has to deal with and of the personal and social problems which have got them where they are. Before she became a doctor she was at the London School of Economics (in the days of Harold Laski) and I am sure that she believes she is fulfilling an essential public duty, from which expediency and authoritarian pressure would be unable to deflect her if she discovered that an injustice was being done on some unfortunate inmate.

Yet somehow this lady has got hold of the idea that membership of a small left-wing theatre club is tantamount to the sort of public political involvement that any civil servant, quite rightly, is not permitted. She is therefore depriving herself of a type of entertainment which she enjoys very much. Who gave her the idea? I am sure that nobody did – in so many words. But there must be an *atmosphere* in the prison that has led her to believe that Unity Theatre is forbidden ground. Lord Stonham's response to the recent complaints about Brixton published in *Peace News* (6 October 1967) was redolent of precisely the same aroma. I can't say I am surprised: but even though one may not be surprised, it is still consistent to be shocked.

# Politics and Police

## 1969

The damage to the Belfast water supply, and the threats against the Prince of Wales's mini-coronation, though serious enough in themselves, do not, I think, justify the Government falling victim to the sort of 'Celto-Phobia' that Livy reports in Rome at the time of the Gaulish attack on that city. The Roman populace, wrote Livy, told each other horrific tales of the giant size of these Trans-Alpine adversaries, with their wild braided hair, their huge beards, and their incredible battle frenzy.

The stories, as usual, proved exaggerated: after one serious defeat, the Romans succeeded in sustaining the shock of the invasion, the Gauls in due time settled down north of the Apennines, and eventually gave birth to the poets Virgil and Catullus – and, at a later remove, to Miss Capulet and Mr Montagu ...

Nevertheless, there is apparently a policy in force on the Euston-Holyhead railway that is at present quite unmodified by any study of Livy's *later* chapters. Recently, I travelled by this route to Ireland. Though not of giant size, I was bearded and unkempt, and my clothes were somewhat casually arranged. I was carrying an over-full briefcase, and a suitcase with a broken handle tied up with string. I was tired and a little flustered, having had – as they say – a bad day. I woke in the middle of the night at Holyhead, and began to stagger from train to ship, thinking only of getting to sleep again as soon as possible.

At the entrance to the dock, I was startled to be intercepted by a detective-officer, of, I believe, the Special Branch. He was by no means an ordinary copper – no bear-like Barlow or terrier Lestrade – but a blond, sneering, cold-eyed young man with a carefully-trimmed fringe-beard. He looked as though he had been trying to impersonate Ralph Schoenman for the purpose of convicting Bertrand Russell. He asked me to 'identify myself'. I complied. He did not appear to believe me. He then proceeded to question me for twenty minutes: about my way-of-life, my politics, my previous convictions, my education.

Having once before been mistaken by a policeman on a railway station for a real wanted man (a kidnapper whose face had been in all the papers) I thought this might be something of the same sort, and so was fairly co-operative to start with. But then the *politics* bit came in: and then a vague reference in his questioning to the Caernarvon Investiture and the Ulster troubles. My replies to his questions got rather frosty. I showed him an out-of-date passport I happened to have with me. This apparently convinced him that I was who I said I was. But even then he asked me the purpose of a trip I had made to Italy in 1954! And even as he apologised for detaining me so long, and said I could now go on board the ferry, he sneered in disbelief.

It was altogether a very strange experience, and one that resulted, I am convinced, from the fact that, since I live in a very wild place with few amenities, I have not shaved for three months. I wonder what he would have done with me had I been wearing a horned helmet?

# A Socialist Hero on the Stage

*Dramatising the Life and Work of James Connolly*
*(Written in collaboration with Margaretta D'Arcy)*

1976

## History and Theatre: Two Techniques

(*a*) 'In the royal town of Edinburgh
    That stands so dark and tall
    There's many a mouse and many a rat
    Live deep in a narrow hole:
    And many a boy and many a girl
    Observe them as they crawl
    Between the cradle and the bed
    And up and down the wall.

    In eighteen hundred and sixty-eight
    In a dark and smoky hole
    In Edinburgh town a child was born
    Who was both pale and small . . .'

(*b*) 'This book is the story of James Connolly's political life and
public activity. It is not the story of his personal affairs or
inner emotions . . . Every effort has been made to check all
details from original sources and, generally speaking, surmises of probabilities are clearly indicated as such . . .

    When Edinburgh first became the capital of Scotland it
consisted of a row of wooden houses perched on the heights
of Castle Hill . . . The tenement system was early established . . . (until) the lower tier of the old town . . . presented

an amazing spectacle. In this melting pot of occupations and
origins, overcrowding, filth, squalor, poverty, drunkenness
and disease were illuminated by flashes of philanthropy,
heroism and revolt ... On October 20, 1856, two twenty-
three-year-old members of the Irish community, John Connolly and Mary McGinn, who lived at 6, Kingstables ...
under the shoulder of Castle Hill ... were married according to the rites of the Catholic Church.'

Quotation (*a*) is from the second scene of Part One of our *Non-Stop
Connolly Show*. It is the beginning of a ballad sung by the actor
who plays John Connolly, father of our central character James.
When he finishes the ballad, the actor playing his son enters, and is
immediately seen setting out with his mother to look for his first
job, which proves to be that of a 'devil' in an Edinburgh printing-
office. Quotation (*b*) is made up of excerpts from the preface and
chapter one of *The Life and Times of James Connolly* by C. Des-
mond Greaves – the standard biographical work. We have set these
passages side-by-side in order to give some idea of the difference
between composing a play about a famous historical character and
writing an accurate and analytical biography. Ourselves and Mr
Greaves have started from much the same place, and with approximately the same point of view – but with quite distinct techniques
and associated responsibilities. The historian must – as Mr Greaves
points out – 'check all details from original sources' and involve
himself as little as possible in 'surmises of probability'. If he quotes
from speeches or conversations he must give chapter and verse for
them and be prepared to prove to his readers that these exact words
were in fact spoken on the specific occasions by the persons to
whom they are attributed. 'Personal affairs or inner emotions' can
only be described if there is absolute evidence for them in the available documents. In any case, Mr Greaves's book is deliberately
stated at the very beginning to be a political rather than a psychological account of his subject. His purpose is to explain why and
how Connolly came to the opinions he did upon matters of public
policy: what action he took as a result of those opinions: and the

subsequent historical meaning of that action. The ultimate effect of such a biography should be not only an addition to the general sum of information about human society; but also – and from the point of view of a Marxist historian, perhaps more importantly – an assistance and inspiration to the activity of Socialists both now and in the future. We do of course hope that the ultimate effect of our plays on the same theme will be very much the same, but one crucial difference must be borne in mind from the very beginning.

As soon as an actor appears on a stage in front of an audience and is understood to represent such-and-such a character, it is immediately obvious to all that this is a *fiction*. He is only pretending. Even though the particular words he speaks may be an exact rendering of words spoken by a real historical personage, the conditions of their delivery have so little in common with the circumstances in which they originated that they too become a *fictional* creation – they have been selected by the playwright and placed in a new context, not the least significant part of which is the presence of the audience. The simple phrase 'I feel ill' whispered by a man to his wife as they sit beside the fire in their private house becomes altogether something else if it is uttered by an actor to an actress on a thirty-foot wide stage in a simulated undertone that is none the less loud enough to be heard by four hundred people. The words are not *fictional* in the sense of being *false*: but if they are true, they are not so much the *real truth* as a reconstructed *emblem* of it. It may be thought that all this species of argument is very elementary and need not nowadays be put before intelligent persons – indeed it was definitively handled by Dr Johnson as long ago as 1765:

> [The spectators] come to hear a certain number of lines recited with just gesture and elegant modulation. The lines relate to some action, and an action must be in some place; but the different actions that complete a story may be in places very remote from each other; and where is the absurdity of allowing that space to represent first Athens and then Sicily which was always known to be neither Athens nor Sicily but a modern theatre? By suppo-

sition, as place is introduced, time may be extended; the time required by the fable elapses for the most part between the acts;
for, of so much of the action as is represented, the real and poetical
duration is the same ... In contemplation we easily contract the
time of real actions and therefore willingly permit it to be contracted when we only see their imitation. It will be asked how the
drama moves if it is not credited. It is credited with all the credit
due to a drama ... Imitations produce pain or pleasure, not because they are taken for realities, but because they bring realities
to mind ...

If we seem to labour the point here it is because the particular genre
of modern theatre into which *The Non-Stop Connolly Show* may
be thought to fall (i.e. the department of Socialist Realism) tends to
be criticised from rather different standards than the ordinary
overtly-fictional *entertainment* play, or even the *uncommitted fine-
art* production: and we are anxious to show that the principles of
all drama are the same, whatever the material involved.

## Dramatic Conflict in the Life of Connolly

The basic theme of theatre is Conflict. A struggle between persons
becomes interesting to an audience by reason of the passions and
*inner emotions* it gives rise to, and the skill of the dramatist is
traditionally shown in the way he or she relates the action of the
struggle to the portrayal of the personal passions. James Connolly, as
a Socialist activist familiar with the ideas of Karl Marx, was impregnated with a philosophy that assumes the class-position of any
individual to be the mainspring of his or her activity, and the mode
of production within any society to be the determinant of its class-
relationships. The obvious actions of his life, when considered with
a view to their translation into the fictional terms of the stage, are
not at first sight particularly dramatic. In other words, his passions
were chiefly moved, not by what happened to him as an individual,
but by the success or failure of the working-class to organise, by the
politico-economic connections between Great Britain and Ireland,
by the problems of running a revolutionary party or producing a

weekly newspaper with inadequate resources. He was not an adulterer, he did not fight duels, he did not get drunk, he did not run mad. The joys and sorrows of his private life, though no less poignant than anyone else's, were not the motivating force for the deeds of his public life. He was to be seen most of the time sitting in a shabby office writing and writing on innumerable sheets of paper, standing on a public platform making speeches to frequently dull assemblies of people, at table in a committee-room conducting tedious and repetitive discussions about trade-unions, manifestoes, programmes and policies.

The conflict of his life was on the whole *impersonal* – it is only to be discovered in the conflict between his class (the working class) and the classes which oppressed it. Only in the last few days of his life did this conflict become *personal and visible* – he took up arms against the British Empire, fought a battle in the streets of Dublin, and died as a result. There is no doubt that the events of Easter 1916 are as immediately suited to the requirements of the stage as, say, the Battle of Agincourt or the Siege of Troy : and neither Shakespeare nor Euripides would have had much doubt as to how to deal with them. But what about the rest – the whole lifetime of forty-eight years which has somehow to be indicated before the figure of James Connolly, war-leader of the Irish Citizen Army, can be properly understood? At one stage, indeed, when we contemplated the task of preparing a whole series of plays about this man (as opposed to one single play, which had been our original idea) we felt so daunted that we had to make up a little rhyme to encourage ourselves:

> My name it is James Connolly
> I neither smoke nor drink :
> Come to the theatre for twenty-six hours
> And watch me sit and think ...

We would not have felt this difficulty so acutely had we been engaged on a television series. The photographic media are basically naturalistic, and a great deal of visual interest can be consistently maintained from exactly the sort of images we have listed above, small in scale, quiet, static, and communicating the intimate details of the man's working routine to the intimate audience that watches him. A film scenario too can offer this sense of enclosed naturalism, but it also gives the opportunity for vast contrasting panoramas – in this case they would obviously be of strike and riot, slum tenements and teeming factories, in the manner of Eisenstein perhaps. The class conflict, in fact, can be demonstrated on a film as a true movement of masses – we mean, that the audience can actually *watch the masses move*. This is not possible in the theatre. The theatre depends for its effectiveness on the physical action of human beings – but not too many of them at one time – it inevitably coarsens the more delicate actions, and reduces the scale of communal activity. If the action to be dealt with is internal (as with Connolly developing the logic of his political theory) or oblique (as with Connolly organising a strike, where the main action would often be in fact non-existent – i.e. the workers are *abstaining* from work – and the protagonist and antagonist would be a committee of management and a committee of workers from one particular factory with Connolly little more than a figure in the background) then direct confrontations between hero and villain become less and less convenient.

It may be argued that this kind of theatre is precisely what the modern stage has specialised in ever since the innovations of Chekhov. But Chekhov was dealing specifically with an area of Russian middle-class life where strong action for defined goals seemed impossible, and a general sense of futility pervaded the entire milieu. Connolly's life was conducted in the very cockpit of the twentieth century, under the gathering storm of the working-class and nationalist struggle that was building up to the first World War and the Russian Revolution. Violence was implicit in every statement, every meeting, every combination of individuals that took place in his environment. It was inconceivable that a dramatic treatment of such a man should not reflect in physical imagery this perpetual class-passion, and the huge movement of class-forces. What Eisenstein provided in his large-scale film-histories had somehow to be suggested by means of a radically different artistic vocabulary. We decided that the only way to handle it was to make a virtue of its very difficulties. If the rage of Connolly against the Capitalist Monster (as he repetitively termed it) was for long expressed only in the minutiae of party-caucus-meetings and inter-union bickerings, then these small-scale events would have to be treated as though they were dynastic quarrels of Renaissance princes in Jocobean tragedy. If, as we discovered from our reading, his years in the USA were dogged by a perpetual inability to see eye-to-eye on politics with the American Socialist De Leon, then we would dramatise this feud (which at first glance in Mr Greaves's book seemed belittling, unworthy of a vigorous 'hero') as though it were, say, the quarrel between the rulers of the world in *Antony and Cleopatra*. Marcus Antonius and Octavius Caesar fought for mastery of the Empire with legions and massed galleys: De Leon and Connolly manipulated committee minutes and wrote letters to party journals. But the passions in both cases were equally huge – and so were the issues.

The Socialist parties in the early 1900s were comparatively obscure on the field of world affairs: but their purpose was nothing less than the turning of the whole world upside-down in the interest of the entire future of the human race – and in a few years they had done it: we were in no doubt that the drama to reflect this must be built on a traditionally heroic scale. We found out very quickly that the essential Conflict of the fable, which ostensibly was that between Capital and Labour, seemed often lost in the tributary struggle between opposed factions of the latter: and that this struggle in itself could time and again be summarised as the Fight between Revolution and Reform – an archetypal *agon* for the dramatist, comparable to such emblematic battles as *Carnival v. Lent*, *Sacred v. Profane Love*, *Idleness v. Industry* et cetera. *Capital v. Labour* is the overall context for the secondary conflicts, and becomes the war between *Evil and Good* or *Darkness and Light* or *Winter and Summer*. It is, as it were, the scenario for late-medieval morality-play. Every time the Revolutionist Cause (Connolly's cause) gained ground, the Capitalist lost ground: whenever the Reformists succeeded in muffling a Revolutionary demand,

Capitalism was made the more secure in its stronghold. It was this repetition of political theme that eventually decided us to write six plays about Connolly instead of just one, and to present them non-stop in one vast theatrical 'event'.

Our original notion had been that the Rising of Easter 1916 would occupy the last act and perhaps most of the middle act of a conventional three-act play, and that it would not be necessary to show the earlier part of Connolly's life in more than a few short, sharp scenes to illustrate his political progress up to the outbreak of the World War. This would have concentrated the main interest of the play upon his decision to bring the Citizen Army into military alliance with the Irish Volunteers under Padraic Pearse : and the main area of argument would have been the rival claims of Nationalism and Socialism. But this argument proved to be only another guise for the Reform versus Revolution controversy; and we felt that none of its earlier manifestations (such as the row between the Irish Socialist Republican Party and Keir Hardie over Connolly's 'treasonable' support for the Boers in the South African War; or the frantic attempts of Connolly and Larkin to gain official British Trade-union help in the Dublin General Strike of 1913) deserved to be curtailed so abruptly as would be needful to squeeze them into a three-act play. At the same time we felt that the inconclusive nature of most of the controversies Connolly had taken part in prior to 1914 was dramatically significant. Nearly all the questions posed in these debates (e.g. the position of Northern Irish Protestant Trade-unionists vis-à-vis the nationalist element of Liberty Hall, Dublin) are not resolved, even today : and the very tediousness and seeming hopelessness of the eternal wrangling was in itself so essential a part of the life-pattern of any Revolutionist, that we could neither omit it nor slide over it too briefly. If we did, we would be in danger of distorting our work into spectacular 'high-theatre' at the expense of the long-drawn 'continuous struggle' which inevitably precedes the actual outbreak of Revolution. Connolly, in fact, had worked very hard with little thanks and no apparent reward throughout his adult life; and it would have been a kind of insult to his memory to fail to present his toil as the chief matter of our story. For these difficulties, at first, we found no solution . . .

## Irish and Indian Experiences

The idea of writing a play about Connolly had first occurred to us in 1969. We had already lived in County Galway for eight years – off and on – but this particular year (just after the outbreak of the present troubles in Northern Ireland) we found ourselves for the first time actually involved to a degree in local affairs. Margaretta D'Arcy had been making an 8mm documentary film of life in the district – originally with no particular purpose in mind save to enlarge her own understanding of the community (Oughterard, near Loch Corrib, and its environs) – and she discovered as she talked to people that under the peaceable and contemplative exterior of the Connacht countryside there were several explosive controversies powerfully on the boil. One of these concerned the question of land-use in the area – should a certain acreage of good arable land which had come on the market be bought by a consortium of hotel-owners and tourism-entrepreneurs to be made into a golf-course, or should it be apportioned by the National Land Commission among a number of small farmers whose own holdings had far too much bog and rock to be economically viable? To support their cause in this and other disputes, the small farmers formed a Civil Rights group (taking cue from the northern Catholics). D'Arcy interviewed the founders of this for her film. Then she joined it herself, and took part in meetings where the political struggle in the North was consciously related to events in the 26 Counties. Her film imperceptibly became a piece of local agit-prop, attacking the gombeen plutocracy of the neighbourhood.

At this time the works of Connolly, whose *martyrdom*, since 1902, had undergone a process of bourgeois Catholic mystification, and whose *ideas* had been subject to deliberate neglect, were once again being published by various left-wing groups. One of these little books, *The Best of Connolly*, edited by Proinsias Mac Aonghusa, was prefaced by a short biography. We read this, and decided that the history of the one representative of Revolutionary International

Socialism among the leaders of 1916 was undoubtedly the most important possible theme for an Irish play of the present day. Mr Mac Aonghusa's biographical notes were nearly as extensive a supply of source-material as any Elizabethan dramatist would have been likely to obtain from his Plutarch or Holinshed: but they were not quite enough for a piece of modern political theatre, where ideologies must be explored and sophisticated economic contradictions exposed. Just then, however, we were busy making preparations for a trip to India, and we put the idea of Connolly on the long finger.

We had been invited to India, in what was the centenary year of the birth of Mahatma Gandhi, by Mr Satish Kumar, a member of the Gandhian non-violence movement. He hoped, and, at the time, we also hoped, that a play by western dramatists on the life and work of Gandhi might prove of some value in both the West and the East: but we needed to see for ourselves. In India we visited a number of Gandhian communities, and had long discussions with workers there about the social and political programme of the movement. We also ran into the Maoist Revolutionaries of Calcutta and elsewhere – the Naxalites – who held a policy in Bengal of armed peasant revolt on Chinese lines, through which 'the capitalist strongholds of the industrial cities might soon be induced to crumble'. This cataclysm has not, yet, materialised: but in 1969–70 its possibility was certainly causing severe apprehension to the authorities. We recognised, between the Naxalites and the Gandhians, the same Revolution versus Reform tensions which obtained throughout the career of Connolly.

We were privileged to meet Mr J. P. Narayan, a distinguished Gandhian activist (later to be imprisoned without trial by the Indian Government). He was already concerned by the apparent failure of his movement to forestall through non-violence the threatened revolt of the Maoist peasantry. He talked to us at some length on these matters, laying the blame for the situation on the refusal of Indian social democracy to redeem its pledges of radical land reform and incorruptible administration. We considered what shape a play about Gandhi could take, in the light of these contemporary developments. Gandhi had been the founding father of Indian social democracy : he had believed that man's will to virtue would overcome the greed of the possessing classes : and if he had so fundamentally miscalculated the ability of individual moral purpose to achieve permanent social change, how could we manage to handle him as a positive dramatic character? We were not interested in dealing with him 'negatively' – i.e. in writing the portrait of an historical failure, or merely in debunking a plaster saint. We had already come to the conclusion that the 'flawed hero' is not a *sine qua non* of 'artistic' theatre, whatever Shakespeare and Sophocles may have made of him in the past,* and whatever Aristotelian prejudices still inform the judgement of contemporary critics.

* In this context we would like to quote from George Thomson's *Marxism and Poetry*: 'Tragedy is a specifically European form of drama. It appears in ancient Athens, and again in western Europe with the rise of the modern bourgeoisie ... [In both of these communities] money-making has now become an end in itself. The merchant goes on and on reinvesting his capital, until eventually – perhaps because other merchants have been playing the same game – he overreaches himself and is ruined ...' The 'flawed hero' in fact is a symptom of a social order in which all power grows out of the strongbox of a bank: and all banks willy-nilly are liable to break. There is no reason why this syndrome should be attributed to a *revolutionary* hero. Shakespeare's protagonists, for instance, are men of position according to the normal standards of his time – Macbeth is a nobleman, Hamlet a prince, Lear a king, Othello a general, and so on. He does not write about rebels in the precise *political* sense. 'Rebels against their own destiny' is a quite different concept. The nearest approach to a conventional tragic hero we came to in the Connolly plays was William Martin Murphy, the archetypal Dublin boss. We gave him a formal, archaic style of verse (hinting perhaps at such 'overweening' characters as Marlowe's Mortimer or Chapman's Bussy):

'By knowing when to sell and when to buy
When to combine and when to destroy
I have enlarged myself into my present size.
Down any street in Dublin cast your eyes:

## Connolly seen as one among several Protagonists ?

Our first solution to this dilemma was to write a series of plays
about a number of historical characters, each of whom had been involved in some sort of revolutionary process of change, or at any
rate an attempt at one. We cannot remember the full list, but it
certainly included Jesus, Gaius Marius, Gandhi, Connolly, Queen
Lakshmi of Jhansi, William Longbeard (the twelfth-century London populist), Toussaint l'Ouverture, Rosa Luxenburg and (as a
comic pendant) the Little Tailor who 'slew seven at one blow'. But
we never really sorted out the exact roster of persons to be dramatised – all we did determine was that each story in the cycle should
contrast with and reflect certain aspects of all the others, and that the
whole thing, when put together, should have something of the
quality of the large-scale Hindu mystery-plays we had been witnessing in various parts of India.

These, although in very variant styles according to the locality
of their performance and the status of the actors (sometimes high-
caste Brahmins, sometimes out-caste tribal people, and so forth),
shared certain overall theatrical concepts – extreme formality mixed
with unexpectedly coarse realism; highly-decorative costumes, make-
up and/or masks, with small relation to everyday naturalism; the
regular use of music and dance as part of the dramatic structure;
strongly rhythmical verse-narrative to link passages of action; very
little in the way of Aristotelian *climax*; and, perhaps above all, a
feeling between actors and audience that the persons and events of

---

Much, if not all, of what you see
In that august perspective belongs to me . . .
I won this round but cannot win again.
The battle now must shift from the foothills to the great wide plain.
You –

    (*He is addressing an allegorical 'War Demon'*)

    – are now called forth by me and mine
And set to work across this world unhindered . . .'

Murphy is the only capitalist figure with whom Connolly comes into
anything like direct confrontation, in Part Five of the cycle, and is
therefore seen as a regular stage-Antagonist.

the drama were something more than the 'historical fictions' we are accustomed to in the western theatre – that they *had been*, still *were*, and *would be* in the future. As the main characters are divine, of course, this last concept is not very surprising, and no doubt it was present in the ancient Greek theatre or the medieval Christian cycles. It is in fact the traditional magic of Dionysus, by which the mask the actor assumes brings with it the real spirit of the person it is an emblem of. Naturalism in recent centuries has so diluted this concept that we feel that even to mention it in serious Socialist circles will give rise to suspicion: but without it, we believe, there is virtually no purpose in the theatre at all. It does not necessarily have anything at all to do with 'religion' in the usually accepted sense of the word: it is a technical phenomenon peculiar to the stage – now in eclipse in the European civilisation of alleged rationality – and has considerable relevance to the political concept of 'continuity of struggle'. If 'the failure of a revolution is the springboard of the next success' and if the ideas of a man like Connolly still live, though he himself has been killed and his party fragmented, then on the stage it should be possible to 'resurrect' him for a few hours as a real living speaking acting human force, not just an 'imitation'. Actors frequently feel that that is exactly what is happening: but the manner of production too often ensures that their subjective sensation is not fully communicated to the audience. The Hindu theatre preserves this effect, not because the people are believing Hindus, but because they have developed a style of writing and presenting the plays which makes it impossible for even non-believers like ourselves to ignore the temporary manifestation of divine forces upon the stage. Between 'divine force' and 'human force' the gap, for the artist, is negligible.

Anyway, on our return to Ireland after a year in the East, we set about the new project. We decided that as so much political action was going on in Ireland, we ought to leave Jesus and Gaius Marius and all the rest of the troop aside for a while, and make a start with James Connolly. A short play, we hopefully thought, which could be presented by itself, by perhaps a company of our own, if we could form one, and be taken on tour to various places throughout the country. If it worked, we could write other plays, one at a time, and add them to the repertory. Each play, when the whole thing was finished, could be performed separately, or the whole lot could be done as a big sequence. We would avoid any sort of archaeological precision in dressing the characters – there would be standard types who would recur in play after play and would be made recognisable each time by their stock marks and costumes. Thus, the Prime Minister Asquith in the Connolly episode might turn up, in the same gear, as Pontius Pilate in the Jesus play, or Napoleon in the Toussaint l'Ouverture story. By the same token, certain scenes from each play would be constructed so as to repeat very similar business and stage-imagery from the other plays. Judas betrays Jesus, Eoin MacNeill puts an advertisement in the newspaper cancelling the Easter Rising, Gaius Marius is rebuffed by the Governor of Carthage . . . and so on.

## Some Political Experience

But all these formal notions remained very vague. Indeed, as we concentrated on Connolly, we gradually began to forget about the other characters, and the cycle receded more and more to the back of our minds. We first had to provide ourselves with more material on Connolly than Proinsias Mac Aonghusa had been able to print. We began with two books, Greaves's biography, and T. A. Jackson's short Marxist history, *Ireland Her Own*. While we were endeavouring to assimilate into theatrical terms the immense complication of incident and political association described by these writers, we became personally involved in Irish politics in the area where we lived. The Civil Rights Committee had taken up the cause of a widow who was facing eviction: the campaign for her defence was also contributed to by the Republican Movement (the Official Sinn Fein Party – at that time reorganising itself upon Socialist principles after the split-away by the Provisionals, and commencing for the first time a regular left-wing electoral strategy in the 26 Counties). For a time, and because it was the only party to relate the eviction case to the overall political position in the country, we became members; and there can be no doubt that we gained quite an understanding of the process of political organisation. Arden, at any rate, confesses to having hitherto skipped over passages in history books that read like this quotation from Greaves:

> Yates replied that there was vilification on both sides. Since he went to Glasgow in 1900 the branch had increased its membership from 6 to 70 or 80, and they had held 400 propaganda meetings. After a lengthy discussion Yates's expulsion was upheld by 56 votes to 6. The resolution furthermore prescribed expulsion without right of appeal for anybody else who 'adopted the conduct or tactics for which G. S. Yates was expelled' ... A special meeting of the Scottish Council was called on the Wednesday after the conference, where it was agreed to report the events of the conference to all Scottish branches at a special delegate meeting on the following Thursday, April 21. When the meeting took place, Geddes was in the chair and it was decided on the motion of Drummond to withdraw from the SSF and establish a new party ...

He would have been inclined to note down the sense of such paragraphs merely as 'trouble in the Scottish Socialist Federation over someone called Yates': and leave it at that.

But attendance at a few branch meetings in Galway filled with 'vilification on both sides' demonstrated to him, as a playwright, in a way that nothing else could, just how much real history can emerge from such apparently futile bickerings. Also, the very obscurity of local branch meetings of a minority political party indicated so clearly the extraordinary tenacity of a man like Connolly, who spent year after year in exactly that environment, and yet was able to draw from it the strength to sustain his Socialist principles in 1914, when every dream of international working-class solidarity seemed a mockery and an illusion. D'Arcy divined a basic image for his character on which we could build the play (neither of us can get down to writing dialogue unless we first have one basic image or analogy in our mind for the chief action of the story) – she saw him as 'The Little Tailor' whom no one takes seriously, but who waddles on through the forest of giants, resourceful and cunning, and eventually succeeds in winning the hand of the princess. Connolly of course 'failed': but insofar as he had placed the Socialist vision firmly into the tradition of Irish revolution (hitherto a primarily nationalist concept) we regarded his life as a triumph: what he did can be built upon, and the principles he discerned need never be invalidated. We had now a degree of understanding, between us, as to the general shape and 'flavour' of the play.

## Some American Experience

At the beginning of 1973 we were invited to America, to the Davis Campus of the University of California, to do a project in the Drama Department. We decided to utilise this visit for the completion and performance of the 1903–1910 section of the Connolly story, when he himself was living and working in the USA. Connolly's American years seemed rather anomalous to our projected dramatic structure, and we were not sure how to handle them. Could they be adequately summarised in one sequence, or should they perhaps be omitted altogether – except as references in speeches once Connolly gets back to Ireland? The trouble was that we did not really understand exactly what he had been involved in in the USA. The chapters in Greaves seemed to take a good deal for granted about his readers' prior knowledge of American labour history; and we could not find many books in Galway to compensate for our ignorance.

But if we could organise a group of students in Davis to do collective research with us on this subject, and then present a partly-improvised, partly-written set of scenes in the theatre there, we believed we could solve the problem. In the event, we found that the use of the Davis University Library, and the dicussions we held with the students in our projects were very valuable indeed. We discovered that most of them did not even accept that there was such a thing as an American white proletariat still in existence, but our researchers into modern-day unions and labour disputes very soon proved otherwise. We made contact with members of the Campus non-academic staff, who were making enormous efforts to unionise the university workers – against very great odds. The Government of California, under Ronald Reagan, would not recognise such organisation for state employees, and the Regents of the University were largely representative of the biggest business interests in the State. Thus an atmosphere of hostility prevailed, not only towards the combination of campus-employees, but also – among many of the academic staff – towards the very nature of our project. It became apparent that difficulties were being put in the way of our work.

Students were mysteriously not available at the rehearsal hours for which we had been assured they would be made entirely free. And a surprising number, having attended one or two sessions of the work, disappeared from sight. A young woman from a different department was always present at the meetings of our group, writing everything down in a notebook, in furtherance of some vaguely-defined 'thesis' of her own: she took care never to contribute to the discussions she so assiduously attended. We became very paranoiac about her (this was the time of the Angela Davis case) – and, as she had never formally obtained our permission for what she was doing (nor had any tutor obtained it on her behalf) we had to tell her to go away. We were informed by the Head of the Department that we should not have done this: it was an infringement of her right to a personal choice, or something. We told him we thought she was somebody's spy, and that was that. In the end we reckoned that we had no chance of getting the small group that was left to us actually on stage in a proper performance about Connolly – there was still far too much elementary preparation to be done.

But we did manage to present an eight-hour sequence of improvised plays, with songs, sketches and films, on the history of American Labour. Most of this was made up of what we called *Henry Dubbs* – from a cartoon character who appeared in the pages of one of the Socialist Party of America's newspapers about the time of the First World War, dug out by D'Arcy from the Reference Library. Dubb was the archetypal non-unionised chauvinist 'backward worker' – a sort of transatlantic Alf Garnett – and we brought his adventures up to date in terms of California in the 1970s. For these playlets we developed a brand of political *commedia dell'arte*, with a consistent use of type-masks. Dubb, for instance, was played by different actors in different sketches: but he always wore the same mask. Likewise the boss-figure, Mr Grab-itall (a name taken from the old cartoon), appeared always in a stock-mask, though he sometimes represented a Regent of the University, sometimes a General of the US Army, sometimes President Nixon ... Part of the show consisted of an 8mm film which D'Arcy made of working-life on the campus, and which was an overt recruiting plea for the campus-workers' union. Many of the group involved in the show were not students from our official 'class' at all, but were union activists or adherents of one of the small Socialist groups to be found, with difficulty, in Davis.

The academic staff, who had brought us to Davis in the first place, boycotted our show almost completely. It was as though, once they had found out the detailed nature of our project and recognised its implications for the time in which they lived (i.e. Angela Davis time; Nixon Second Inauguration time; very nearly Uncovering of Watergate time), they were anxious to forget that we even existed in their Drama Department ... Ironically enough, though, this very abandonment of our project by the authorities gave us a much greater freedom to experiment than we would otherwise have had ...

## Practical Possibilities

When we got home again to Ireland we had found out a lot about Connolly in America and also written several scenes from his early life. It is always a practical course of action with any new play to secure the interest of some company or producer before one starts writing, and – if possible – to obtain a commission and money-in-advance. Not only does this help one to earn a living from work *written* as opposed to work *performed*, but it also provides the needful stimulus of a deadline to get words onto paper and to cut too much rumination. In 1971, Arden had already been approached by the BBC for a radio play as a commissioned work. If he sent a subject and title to them, for recording in the files, a contract would immediately be dispatched for him to sign. He replied that he wanted to write on the theme of what he then called 'Connolly in 1916' – and he would do it in collaboration with D'Arcy. (As an Englishman he felt nervous about handling Irish material without an Irish partner – in any case it had been D'Arcy who originally conceived the Connolly idea.) The BBC dropped the commission like a hot brick. A play on such a subject, they said, might 'inflame passions in Northern Ireland', where, we were reminded, the broadcasts were heard. Well, the play was not written for BBC Radio: and the inflamed passions of Ulster have not noticeably been subdued . . .

The next possibility of a definite production for the play came in 1973 from the 7:84 Company. They had already presented an exciting version of Arden's *Serjeant Musgrave's Dance* adapted by John McGrath to the events of Bloody Sunday in Derry, and had produced *The Ballygombeen Bequest* by both authors to considerable critical acclaim. While we were waiting to get our hoped-for company together in Ireland, a British production by this group would be an excellent medium for the knowledge of our current work to be brought across the Channel. There was talk of an Edinburgh Festival presentation later in the year: but on account of various theatrical exigencies, the project fell through. In a way we were relieved that it did, because the play would have had to be completed rather rapidly, and we were not sure that we had sufficiently mastered all the material to do this to our own satisfaction. As it was, we found ourselves suddenly liberated from an imminent deadline; and it was possible to take stock of alternative options.

We then had an unexpected visit from Robert Walker, who was about to take up a post as Director of the Lincoln Repertory Theatre. He had just returned from a period of work in West Germany, where he had been intrigued by an immensely long theatrical epic dealing with the first World War. He was also, at this time, considering the chances of including in his Lincoln programme *Trotsky in Exile* by Peter Weiss – a play of unusual scale which is notable for its intense concentration upon Trotsky's political ideology rather than the more 'personal' themes of his private life. We had already read this work, and, although we did not think that Weiss's technique would exactly lend itself to our own subject-matter, we were stimulated by it. We talked with Mr Walker a great deal about these ideas and political/historical theatre in general. When he left, we immediately began work upon the division of Connolly's life into an appropriate number of parts for the construction of a large dramatic cycle. (We should mention, perhaps, that as we live in a fairly remote part of the West of Ireland, visitors who can talk of recent experiences in the British or European theatre are rare. So when we get one, we tend to react like the inhabitants of an English fishing village in the 1580s who suddenly find a mariner in their midst who has just been round the world with Drake. This visit had had a quite violently catalytic effect on us both.) Our original notion of a cycle of episodes about several different characters was recalled, but now modified into a new scheme of several different episodes from the development of *one* character. The principles of stock-masks, parallel incidents, and non-naturalistic formality of staging were to be retained in the new concept. We then had to consider how much of what should go into each episode.

## The Six-part Cycle

Connolly's political activities, considered with such a degree of year-by-year detail, present certain problems to the dramatist: because much of what he said and did depended on, and can only be explained by reference to, a number of things that were happening outside Ireland altogether. The Paris Commune of 1871, the Boer War, the 1905 Russian Revolution, the expansion of the USA into Latin America and the West Pacific, the militant unionisation of the Colorado miners, the ebb and flow of the Socialist International throughout the whole period – all these events and many more had first to be understood by the playwrights, and then, one way or another, made relevant to the audience. The information was not available in Greaves or Jackson; and before we knew where we were we were surrounded by the history of half of the world over nearly half-a-century. We made vast charts, showing parallel happenings in all the appropriate areas of geography and politics, and stuck them up on the wall of our workroom. But the final decision to include this or that episode in the plays had in the end to be decided by intuition rather than reasoning. You can reason out a history thesis according to established data: but a play has to be constructed through the imaginative grasp of the human probabilities of each individual character.

Connolly's life fell usefully into six epochs; each one made a play. They are:

### Part One: 'Boyhood' 1868–1889

Connolly, born in Edinburgh of poor Irish parents, joins the Army and is posted to Ireland during the Land League agitation. He becomes aware of both nationalism and socialism, falls in love, deserts.

### Part Two: 'Apprenticeship' 1889–1896

Married to Lillie, he lives in Edinburgh and works as a dustman. Joins the Scottish Socialist Federation. Becomes a branch-secretary and fails to win election to the city council. Poverty compels him to look for an appointment elsewhere as a paid political organiser.

### Part Three: 'Professional' 1896–1903

He gets this appointment to the Dublin Socialist Club. Forms the Irish Socialist Republican Party and agitates spectacularly against imperialism. He resigns from the Party after a row over its organisational incompetence, and decides to emigrate to America.

### Part Four: 'The New World' 1903–1910

In America he joins the Socialist Labor Party and soon quarrels with its policy. He resigns, and becomes an organiser for the Industrial Workers of the World. He then moves towards the Socialist Party of America, and for a time works for them at

a reasonable salary. He seems to have accomplished nothing ...
News of a political and trade-union resurgence in Ireland brings
him home again.

## Part Five: 'The Great Lockout' 1910–1913

Larkin has founded the Irish Transport Workers' Union. Connolly is appointed union organiser in Belfast and is involved in
several severe disputes. The Employers' Federation of Dublin
confronts the ITWU with a lockout, which is replied to by
general strike. The Citizen Army is formed to protect the
strikers. The strike finally fails, due to lack of full support from
Britain.

## Part Six: 'World War and the Rising' 1910–1914

The constitutional crisis in Ireland comes to a head just before the
World War breaks out. Connolly stands by the decisions of
International Socialism to mobilise the working class against the
war. But is almost alone in this. He allies himself with the
National Volunteer faction under Pearse, brings the Citizen
Army into the Easter Rising. Is captured and shot.

We completed the scripts towards the end of 1974. We had not
written them specifically for performance in either Ireland or
Britain: but we were aware that the emphasis and meaning of the
plays would be slightly different according to which country they
were to be presented in. So we left ourselves open for re-writing
portions for particular audiences. If the plays were shown in
Ireland, we wished to demonstrate the *internationalism* of Connolly
(in contrast to his traditional image of a national martyr): if in
England, we were more concerned to convey the complexities of
Britain's imperial legacy across the water. In the event, a Dublin
production was the first possibility which offered; and we had to
consider how we should place our work within the existing Irish
theatrical tradition.

## Theatre in Ireland

The fact is, that although Ireland has had many playwrights and actors of the highest quality, there has never been an Irish tradition of *theatre* – in the sense of an all-embracing concept of art or craft which can include within it all the various dramatic activities: writing, performing, singing and dancing, designing décor et cetera, all woven together into one coherent aesthetic. To understand why this is so, we must go back to the Middle Ages. Unlike most of Western Christendom, Ireland had no corpus of native plays in this period. Such Miracle plays, Moralities or Popular Farces as were performed in the country, were in English and were provided for the Anglo-Norman garrisons of the Pale and outlying settlements. The Irish themselves lived either as rural clans or – if they did come under the control of the English crown – in a state of semi-servitude. There was constant guerilla warfare. The stable urban conditions for theatrical development never existed. The arts of the clans (bardic poetry, singing, instrumental music, etc.) were individual rather than group activities and largely oral in technique. There was no religious reformation in the sixteenth century, and therefore no transition (as in England) from the divinely-centred Catholic drama to the secular plays of the 'Shakespearian' Renaissance – which coincided, as is well known, with the first true permanent commercial theatre. Later, in the second half of the seventeenth century and the beginning of the eighteenth, the developed commercial theatre of Great Britain extended itself into Ireland, as an entertainment for the Anglo-Irish Protestant Ascendancy class, and operated entirely in the English manner. Such Irish artists as worked in this theatre, either at home or in Britain, were bound to adopt the artistic conventions of the British tradition. Macklin, Peg Woffington, Sheridan, Barry Sullivan, Wilde and Shaw are names which immediately come to mind. They were all recognised as being identifiably *Irish* in temperament: but the tradition of their working environment remained clearly derived from the Miracle Cycles of York and Coventry, from the Globe Theatre of 1599, from the Restoration playhouses of Betterton and Nell Gwynn.

In the meantime, the defeat of the Irish Catholic peoples in the seventeenth-century wars, and the general exile of their clan-aristocracies, had depressed the native Gaelic culture to the fragmentary cottage celebrations of an impoverished tenantry. Numbers of this class moved into the towns to become an urban proletariat: and by the middle of the nineteenth century they were (when they could afford it) enthusiastic and often riotous playgoers. The repertoire of the theatres they attended was roughly similar to that in London: and naturally included a preponderance of typical Victorian melodrama. But it was frequently *Irish* melodrama. That is to say, instead of the poor but honest Jolly Jack Tar saving his Black-Eyed Susan from the mortgage-foreclosers or the lechery of his superior officer, audiences in Dublin were given the noble Fenian rebel, on the run from the redcoats, being helped to board an American packet-boat by his colleen, so that he could 'scape the gallows and sail to the land of liberty. Dion Boucicault was the best-known of the writers of such plays, though there were many others, not necessarily in business outside Ireland at all. This was, in one sense, Irish theatre for the Irish public: but the style of the presentation and the technique of the playwriting was little different from that to be found in Britain – or America – or anywhere else where the English-language drama had sent out its roots during three centuries of colonial expansion.

Towards the end of the nineteenth century, however, came the Gaelic Revival in Ireland – a reassessment of the native, pre-colonial heritage of the people; parallel to the Slavic Revival in Russia, as well as to many other nationalist assertions all over Europe. It naturally included a movement towards a genuine Irish theatre. The principle exemplar was Ole Bull's work in Norway, where, in addition to establishing the necessity of presenting plays in the hitherto downgraded Norwegian language, he was also able to bring forward two playwrights of unassailably international quality – Björnson and Ibsen. Such writers as W. B. Yeats and Lady Gregory sought to inspire a school of Irish playwriting which need not be ashamed to exist in the same world as Ibsen, while, on the side of acting and production, the Fay brothers began to develop an Irish manner which should express the Irish temperament without recourse to English patterns. They had to hand the Gaelic tradition of improvised narrative and witty repartee; but this was an individual oral form of art, and did not belong to the *theatre* until it was married with some concept of group performance and style. They went to France to find one: and adopted the aesthetic of Antoine's *Théâtre Libre*. This avant-garde director/actor had trained an amateur company in a mode of delicate restrained formality which was at the same time far more *realistic* in its presentation of emotion than the old declamatory tradition of the theatre: and it had an immediate success when applied to such modern authors as Ibsen. The Fays were also attracted by the non-professional aspect of the work. It is significant that they first tried out a similar method with a women's cultural group in Dublin known as *Inginidhe-na-hEireann* (The daughters of Ireland) which was set up by Maud Gonne. She was a militant nationalist and associated with the Yeats circle of literary revivalists. She belonged to the Irish Republican Brotherhood, a 'subversive' secret society devoted to the establishment of a Republic by force. In this her political attitude contrasted with that of most of the other people involved in the new theatre movement, who tended to support some form of non-violent devolution – either Home Rule or the Sinn Fein programme of passive abstention from British parliamentary institutions. The Yeats school of playwrights came together with the Fay school of amateur actors to form the Abbey Theatre in 1903. Before this took place, indeed, the Fay actors had already performed a play by Yeats (*Cathleen ni Houlihan*) with Maud Gonne in the leading role. This was an overtly political and romantic appeal to national sentiment, clearly in favour of physical force as a means of liberation. Yeats was later to hope that he had not (with this work) sent men out to die: in fact, of course, he had, and they did . . .

*Cathleen ni Houlihan* was the first of a series of politically-motivated pieces of nationalist agit-prop which continued for many years on the Irish stage. The Abbey – as a theatre – never endorsed such plays as the *sine qua non* of an Irish drama: the programmes included other works which infuriated the nationalists (often for the wrong reasons), and which seemed designed to keep the company in favour with the British authorities of Dublin Castle. Synge's *The Playboy of the Western World* was the best-known of these. Not only at the Abbey, but also on the boards of a number of amateur theatre-clubs (Irish-speaking as well as English) associated with political groups, propagandist drama was to be found. Padraic Pearse was a playwright, so was the Countess Markievicz, so indeed was James Connolly (whose *Under Which Flag?*, attacking recruitment to the British Army and recommending enrolment in the ranks of rebellion, was played by The Workers' Dramatic Company only four weeks before the 1916 Rising). On the whole, the main point about this committed drama was that its revolutionary content was not combined with any innovations of form. There was something of the Ibsen–Antoine tradition, something of the Yeats–Synge Irish poetic style, and a good deal of the old Boucicault heroic melodrama in its make-up. After the Treaty of 1922, the more disillusioned political style of Sean O'Casey appeared – parallel to the early work of Brecht in Germany (compare *The Plough and the Stars* with *Drums in the Night* . . .) – but when this playwright developed into the author of *The Silver Tassie* (a thoroughly European play with little about it that one could call specifically Irish) he was rejected by the Abbey and had to go to England. He was, of course, an international Socialist – he had organised the Citizen Army for Larkin, but had resigned over the growing links of that body with the National Volunteers in 1914. He regarded Connolly as a man who had mistakenly replaced the red flag by the green and thereby betrayed the true cause of the workers. O'Casey's later style owed much to the same German Expressionism that Brecht was to transform into so eloquent a vehicle for Marxist theatrical art.

In England, O'Casey was closely associated with the left-wing Unity Theatre: and a great deal of the vocabulary of English political drama is derived from his example. There was, in the 1930s, some similar work in Ireland, performed by amateurs, and connected with the political Left. In recent years the whole concept of political theatre in the country has been revitalised. The 7:84 Company, on tour in Ireland with plays by John McGrath upon Socialist themes, received very wide acclaim, by no means confined to strictly 'committed' circles, and as much for their theatrical excitement as their ideology. In Dublin Eoghan Harris wrote and presented a play about Connolly's colleague, James Larkin, which was sponsored by the Workers' Union of Ireland – Larkin's union – as an act of commemoration. Eamonn Smullen, Director of Economic Affairs for the Official Sinn Fein Party, has written a play *The Reprisal*, analysing the roots of terrorism by analogy with the agrarian troubles of the 1820s. This has been given public readings, though not (at the time of writing) a full production. These examples, it will be seen, are all from the 'fringe' of the Irish theatre. There was a possibility that a modern political complexion might be given to the more *established* stage, when Lelia Doolan (who had resigned from the national television service upon grounds of political principle) was appointed to be artistic director at the Abbey in the early seventies; but she soon found her sense of radical commitment incompatible with the atmosphere in that building, and resigned within less than two years. In 1974 various meetings were organised in Dublin to discuss the foundation of a regular Socialist theatre company: but so far the idea is unrealised.

Granted then the existence of at least *this* tradition, that in Ireland the theatre is expected to be used for political purposes, and granted that there is no specifically Irish style or manner of dramatic *production* even today, we had to decide, if the plays about Connolly were to be done in Dublin, at whom they should be aimed and how far should the content determine the form, or vice versa. It was not credible that plays on this subject and on so large a scale could be produced in the ordinary context of Irish middle-class theatre practice. The hand-to-mouth ad hoc state of the acting profession would alone have made this unworkable. Through discussion with a number of interested people, D'Arcy arrived at the idea of a kind of giant 'pop festival' for the Left – a long night of plays, films, etc. in some central and easily accessible locality, with fairly cheap seats, and an overall atmosphere of unity and solidarity. The *Angry*

*Arts* weeks in New York and London during the Vietnam War provided the impulse for this concept. Our plays would be aimed directly at audiences of Socialists and Republicans.

## Unity and Solidarity ?

The inability of the Abbey management, even in its earliest days, to satisfy all its public at once with a genuine 'national' philosophy of art only reflected the enormous gulfs of ideology and socio-political purpose which still divide the Irish people. Leaving out of the argument for the time being the effects of a half-century of National Partition on those in the North, let us look at a few statistics of opinions held by a sample of post-primary school-children south of the Border who were questioned in 1972. As junior citizens of the 26-County Republic, one might perhaps expect them to have inherited a certain consensus of view upon at least the overall 'aim and purpose' of this independent state, which was created within living memory, and towards the hope of which the sentiments of the founders of the Abbey had been tending in 1902. But in fact the figures betray a widespread confusion, which has little to do with conventional class distinctions. Nearly 70% identi-fied *Ireland* as the whole island. But 25% thought it was the Republic and identified Northern Ireland as a foreign nation. 84% rejected the suggestion that England had always had the best interest of Ireland at heart: yet they were not hostile to the English and thought they were generally good people. 'I'd hate to live in England' cropped up frequently – though not one of them used the word 'hate' about the British government or people. 36% agreed with the statement 'He defends his freedom if necessary with the gun' as a definition of good citizenship, whereas 52% were specifically anti-IRA. 30% thought that in the circumstances of 1972 the violence in the North was necessary. 53% were opposed to the use of force to end British rule there. There seems to be some-thing almost schizoid about such radically diverse opinions on so basic a question as 'What is the Irish nation?' But what else can be expected in a country which contains the extraordinary phenome-non of the Republican Movement?

Socialism in Ireland without Republicanism and Republicanism without Socialism are mirror-image concepts like two lamp-posts in a bog – bright but quite useless. Or, at any rate, so they have hitherto proved. The principles of Socialism are well-enough known everywhere – but Republicanism . . .? There can be few countries in the world where a military, secret-society-type dissident group shares the same national anthem and the same national flag as the regular government it refuses to recognise. The Army Council of the IRA is held by true Republicans to be the real legal government of the 32-County Republic set up by Proclamation in 1916. It was originally a democratic Republic: but during the Civil War the Dail was forced to put elections into 'temporary' abeyance. The Free State party who won the war re-established elections for a 26-County Administration alone: and this, in purist terms, can never be called 'The Republic'. The argument is thoroughly legalistic, and difficult to refute. It may sound as much of a mystical fiction as the more prolonged survivals of the Jacobite Cause; but if it is a fiction it is a fiction that costs lives – and shows no signs of ceasing to do so. How many citizens of the 26 Counties still believe in it (while at the same time voting for the membership of the present Dublin Dail and Senate, if only to keep some sort of representative in office to look after their tax problems or their applications for health certificates or their cousins who want appointments in the post office)? It is impossible to say. The importance of the question is understood by nearly everybody and virtually ignored in public discussion of national affairs. It surfaces from time to time, on occasions such as the banning of a Provisional Sinn Fein march in Dublin for Easter 1976, and the defiance of that ban by thousands. Even then the true issues are disguised by the use of the word 'subversive' to describe the Republican viewpoint. The IRA in this context is neither more nor less subversive than was the House of York in the reign of Henry VI or the House of Lancaster in that of Edward IV. There still exists, in fact, an unconcluded Civil War throughout the whole of Ireland, inseparable of course from the war in the North against imperialism and the heritage of colonial plantation. Its resolution in the South cannot be predicted so long as the North remains in turmoil.

Now, given a society so divided as this one, how can it be expected that any philosophy of theatre can evolve to speak with one voice to the ears of even the 'dissident' community? For not even the Republican Movement itself remains at one. Since the first disastrous split over the Rising of 1916 when Eoin MacNeil was opposed to military action at that particular time, and was outmanoeuvred by Pearse; to the outbreak of Civil War over the Treaty of 1922; to the repudiation of the IRA by de Valera and Fianna Fail in the thirties; to the breakaway of the Provisionals from the Officials in 1970, the internal purging of the Officials in 1972, the consequent formation of the Irish Republican Socialist Party and the internecine feud between these two factions in 1975; the centrifugal succession of events has continued. How could one write even a 'Republican' play which would satisfy each and every one of these tendencies?

We can be sure that such a play would appeal not at all to the Fine Gael voters, whose own political line descends from the Blueshirt Fascists of O'Duffy (supported by W. B. Yeats); from the Free Staters of Cosgrave senior, Arthur Griffith and Michael Collins; from the anti-physical-force Home Rule Parliamentarians; from Daniel O'Connell who secured the Emancipation of Catholics in the epoch of Reform that followed the French Revolution ... Would a play on a 'Republican' theme appeal to Labour? We can be sure it would not appeal to those of the Labour Party at present in Coalition with Fine Gael: but James Connolly was a founder of the Irish Labour Party, and Connolly was a Republican. There are many who share his views in the trade-unions and in the rank-and-file of the Party today. Some of them may also, perhaps, be associated with one or another of the 'subversive' Republican groups. And remember, in Ireland, the Trade-Union Movement is not necessarily all-Labour in its national politics. All over the country union-organisers and shop-stewards are ardent partisans of de Valera's parliamentary 'republican' party of Fianna Fail ... The whole thing is so complicated that we will spare the reader any more of it.

## Production at Liberty Hall

Nevertheless, it proved possible for us to present the Connolly plays in Liberty Hall, at Easter 1975. This was the original 'Workers' Bastille' where the General Strike of 1913 was organised, where the Citizen Army was administered, and whence Connolly marched out to the Post Office on Easter Monday 1916. The building itself, of course, is new : but its function – the HQ of the Irish Transport and General Workers' Union – remains the same. It was this Union who allowed us to use their conference hall for our production, and let us occupy one room or another in the basement of the offices for many weeks of our three months' rehearsal. Our properties and costumes were prepared on an unused upper floor of the HQ of the Official Sinn Fein Party. Without this crucial support from a great trade-union and a Republican political party we could never have hoped to stage the cycle, as the money was simply not available for the hire of premises for anything like the period needed. It must be recorded, furthermore, that at the time of our heaviest work, when we were absolutely dependent upon continuity of rehearsal, and indeed right up to and during the days of performance themselves, these two organisations were in a state of considerable crisis. The Sinn Fein split with the IRSP had come to a head, people had been killed in Belfast, and one of the party central-committee members was shot down outside his own house in Dublin. Their offices were picketed by angry opponents, and an incendiary or bomb attack on the building was for a time a real possibility. The ITGWU meanwhile had to deal with a series of crucial decisions on the National Wage Agreement, and at the same time administer a large number of serious strikes and other disputes in various parts of the country, which of course meant frequent priority-demands on the space which we were using. It is a remarkable tribute to the high value placed upon political theatre by certain individuals in these organisations that we were enabled to continue.

We should mention in particular the support given us by Mr Des Geraghty of the ITGWU and by Mr Eamonn Smullen of Sinn Fein, because without them there would certainly have been no

Connolly plays shown in Dublin that year. Moreover, neither Sinn Fein nor the Union imposed any conditions of censorship upon our script or production. Neither organisation demanded assurances that the political line of the plays would be in accordance with their declared policies. It was simply accepted that Connolly deserved a play : and that it was up to the playwrights to do him such justice as they could. They also agreed (and given the anarchic situation prevailing in the country at the time, it was a noteworthy concession) that members of opposed factions would not be deterred from attending the plays, if they so desired, provided they gave no sign of trying to start a 'provocation'. In fact we had absolutely no trouble of that sort, though some people had been rather scared at the outset.

## Performances and Performers

The cast was made up of :

(*a*) a small nucleus of professional actors hired at Equity- minimum rates. Three of them had to be invited in from England, because the nature of Dublin theatre employment is inimical to any commitment by an artist to an experimental production lasting as long as three months. Outside of the Abbey Company, where the actors are safeguarded with long-term contracts, there is a constant need to accept all work offered when it is offered; so a performer's work-diary tends to be dotted with two-or-three-day television or radio dates booked weeks in advance;

(*b*) members of the Workers' Cultural Group – young trade-unionists who had already presented programmes of Irish music, but had had no experience of theatre. They could only attend rehearsals on certain evenings each week;

(*c*) a considerable number of young people who were either students or in part-time employment. In general they had links with the Dublin 'theatre fringe', or with university drama groups, and some of them intended to become professional theatre-workers.

(*d*) members of the Fianna – 'boy-scouts' of the Republican Movement, originally founded by the Countess Markievicz – aged
approximately nine to twelve.

Our scenic designer and our musical director both came from
England, where they had worked with us before on two of our
plays, and had a thorough understanding of our style. They were
'seconded' to us from the Welfare State Company in Lancashire.

This heterogeneous assembly numbered altogether about fifty
persons; and the rehearsals were co-ordinated by a production team
of four – the authors, Jim Sheridan of Dublin (who brought in the
'fringe-theatre' element of the cast), and Robert Walker from
Britain (who fetched over the other two UK members of the acting
company). Eamonn Smullen and Des Geraghty acted as a kind of
'arbitration tribunal' when any problems arose about the clarity of
the plays or the organisation of the production. Our working-hours
were from ten in the morning till ten at night, every day; so that
each participant's individual time-table could be fitted into the
schedule somewhere.

The performances covered a period of about six weeks. The
whole cycle was staged continuously in Liberty Hall for one major
performance which lasted from Easter Saturday at noon until Easter
Sunday at 2.30 pm. The intervals between the separate parts of the
cycle were occupied by shorter plays from two visiting political
theatre companies, The Red Ladder from Britain, and The Puny
Little Theatre from Dublin. There were also films in these intervals – we do not remember all of them at this remove, but they
included Eisenstein's *Strike* and *The Battleship Potemkin*. A
section of the Workers' Cultural Group sang labour-songs and there
were other singers and instrumentalists. A hot and cold buffet was
supplied by the Catering Section of the ITGWU, and full meals
could be eaten by actors and audience in between sections of the
show.

The following week there were separate performances of each
of the six plays, one per night, in Liberty Hall. After that the plays
were divided into smaller units of about one hour each, and pre-

sented in various locations around Dublin – the two universities, a community centre in the working-class suburb of Ballymun, etc. Smaller units still were put on as street-plays, notably in Moore Street, the main Dublin market area. A reduced company then took the show on tour. Five of the six plays were given in continuous performance in Queen's University, Belfast. This was followed by single episodes for various social clubs in the 'Catholic ghettoes'. We regretted very much that we could not play in Protestant areas as well: but it is a fact of life in Northern Ireland that one cannot move at will from one district to another. We had no contacts with local Loyalist organisers, by whose invitation alone could we have performed in their bailiwicks. We had hoped that the Queen's performance would have been our major 'non-sectarian date', but it was poorly attended. Publicity had been sabotaged by hostile members of the University staff who had incorrectly assumed that a play about Connolly from Dublin must be some sort of endorsement of IRA bombings, and in any case movement about town at night was very difficult at this time because of much killing – the organiser of our visit to Belfast, Mr Liam MacMillen, was shot dead two days after we had left the city. Our other Northern Irish dates were Newry and Downpatrick. We then played five of the plays in Galway. Visits to Cork and Limerick were arranged to follow the Galway trip: but a sudden petrol-distributors' strike made transport impossible, and the dates had to be cancelled.

The publicity for the show in Dublin was initially concentrated in the various political and trade-union newspapers rather than the theatrical columns of the daily press. More general publicity was developed close to the date of the production; but a lengthy feature in *The Irish Times* was printed on the *industrial* page instead of the cultural. This had the effect of indicating the emphasis of the show and was instrumental in bringing in a fair proportion of the sort of audience we felt ourselves to be particularly addressing. Immediately before the doors opened at Liberty Hall on Easter Saturday, some of the cast marched in costume to the beat of a drum up O'Connell Street to the Post Office and round the side streets, carrying banners and some of the large puppets which were to be used in the plays. We don't know whether this archaic 'theatre parade' brought anybody in, but at least it set the show going with a flourish, and gave a clue to the attitude with which we regarded Connolly as a figure for the Dublin stage: we were deliberately setting out to re-create a national – and local (not only the Rising but also the demonstrations and riots of the 1913 Lockout took place in these very streets just round the Post Office) – folk-hero, who has long been enshrined in an iconic portrait, but whose detailed life is not well known, still less his particular political activities and controversies.

## The Content of the Plays

Within the overall concept of Connolly as a man justifiably revered by the Irish working class were many cruxes of political interpretation, which are by no means resolved, and which give rise to considerable heat whenever his work is analysed. The great length of the cycle of plays, and their deliberately repetitive structure, made it possible to dramatise the contradictions and complexities so fully that we felt all the various objections that could be raised by particular factions might be answered by point-ing to at least one of the episodes in the cycle and the argument implied by it. When it came to formulating these arguments, the old problem that always dogs political dramatists came up – how far should we go in 'presenting both sides of the question'? Where the question was one which divided two differing Socialist or working-class points of view we tried to present the principles of Connolly's opponent as strongly as possible. Thus his controversies with Keir Hardie or with William Walker, the Ulster labour-leader, were given at some length and – we believe – with perfect 'fairness'. Where Connolly's answer to a particular objection has not obviously been proven correct by subsequent history, we did not tendentiously endeavour to wrap up the difficulty in unsupported assertions.

Thus, Rosa Luxemburg's attack on nationalist tendencies with-in the international Socialist movement, which is shown in the play taking place at the Paris Conference of 1900, is not properly answered by Connolly. He, as it were, postpones consideration of the problem:

> 'In her place, quite clearly, national sentiment is of small value: but the Irish question's different and we judge it by different rules. The next time we go to one of these international affairs, we are going to have to work out much more thoroughly our particular philosophy and explain it with great care . . .' (Part Three).

In Part Six Connolly has a dream where a giant bird, representing perhaps the voice of Scientific Socialism, half-emerges from a broken eggshell and offers him a list of 'Prohibitions': i.e. the things that ought not to be done by a Socialist Internationalist in a crisis. He is already contemplating doing all these things (collaborating with the nationalist Volunteers; ignoring the reality of working-class Unionism in Ulster; setting a military adventure afoot without a proper basis in the working-class mass-movement, etc.), and he rejects the bird's warning with some attempt at argument – but even at this late stage there is little of what one could call 'dialectical strength'. As readers of history and students of modern politics, we believed that he had no choice but to take part in the Rising: as dramatists we were aware that his decision was questioned then (by O'Casey, for instance) and has frequently been questioned since. We also felt sure that in the terrible tensions of 1916 he must have been activated as much by deep emotion and intuitive response as by any carefully thought out programme of reasoning. So the scene in verse between him and the bird is sandwiched between two prose scenes in which he and the Volunteers argue the pros and cons in a far more 'political' way – but even this argument is conditioned by the desire for both sides to come to the same conclusion: that the Rising must be embarked upon, and that they each need the other in it. The conflicting points of view echo Rosa Luxemburg's warning from Part Three, and have also been stated and re-stated throughout all six plays in a variety of different ways. This is one example of an intertwining arrangement of repeated themes running through all parts of the cycle. (There are many others – we had in mind a sort of dramatic version of the interlacing patterns common to traditional Celtic art, as in the Book of Kells and so forth . . .)

Where we did not choose to show 'both sides of the question with an equal balance' was in dealing with Connolly's prime enemies, Capitalism and Imperialism. We accepted his reasoning that the destruction of these two interconnected systems was a desirable goal, and then concentrated on the problem of 'how to achieve it'. Sergei Eisenstein, writing about his *Ivan the Terrible* films, has explained the principle behind this particular dramatic concept; and if one reads 'Connolly' for 'Ivan' the following quotation fully expresses our attitude:

> Irrelevant details in the characters of the other personages are ignored, while their principle features – chiefly their hostility or loyalty to Ivan's cause – are drawn in bold relief. Because of this, when taken individually, some of the characters may perhaps seem somewhat one-sided. But the point is that they must be taken together as a whole, in their general relationship to the cause for which Ivan stands. They cannot be taken separately, just as the part of one instrument cannot be singled out in judging a whole complex orchestrated score, for the meaning of their individual actions is disclosed only in their general inter-action. Neither can they be considered outside the plastic setting and musical whole in which they are immersed. (*Ivan the Terrible*, edited by Ivor Montague, London, Seeker & Warburg, 1963.)

Overt advocates of Capitalism or Imperialism would therefore find the thesis of our plays unacceptable. We make no apology for this. We do not believe that conditions exist anywhere in the allegedly 'free' world, and least of all in Ireland, for a work of art to be based (as were the mediaeval Miracle plays or the comedies of Aristophanes) upon a philosophical perspective common to the entire society irrespective of social class. Capitalism in our plays is represented by a 'demon king' figure called Grabitall, who wears

the same mask throughout the cycle, but goes under several different names, according to his role in each part of the story. In Part Three, for instance, he is the Lord Lieutenant of Ireland; in Part Four he is Pierpoint Morgan; in Parts Five and Six he is William Martin Murphy. He has three similarly stock-masked henchmen, known as the Employers, who change their nationality and names*
in the same way. Military, ecclesiastical, bourgeois-political, judicial figures are dealt with by means of the same convention. Members of the working-class and national liberation movements, whether for or against Connolly, do not wear masks, but are only given that degree of individuality consistent with the particular needs of their role in the story.

Costumes were colourful and spectacular, not naturalistic. There were big, feathered head-dresses and purple wigs; all military persons wore elaborate scarlet or blue full-dress; Tory aristocrats had grotesque masks like birds of prey; members of Socialist parties wore white shirts, dark waist coats, workers' hats/caps and red neckerchiefs. Connolly alone consistently dressed and was made-up to look like the historical portraits – though there was some attempt at accuracy of *atmosphere* rather than precision of detail about the appearance of such well-known individuals as the Countess Markievicz, Jim Larkin, Padraic Pearse, W. B. Yeats or Maud

---

* The names of two of the Employers are Hook and Crook (when they are English: we call them MacHook and MacCrook in the Scottish scenes and O'Hookey and Crookey for the Irish episodes). These characters had in fact already been employed by us in a script we had collaborated on in 1971 – *Two Hundred Years of Labour History* – written in conjunction with Roger Smith, and at the invitation of the Socialist Labour League (now the Workers' Revolutionary Party), for a rally at the Alexandra Palace. The techniques of political playwriting we developed in the Connolly cycle owed an enormous amount to our experience of this production. D'Arcy was a member of the cast, and has since taken part in another play for the same Party. The WRP, to the best of our knowledge is the only Socialist organisation in the UK to make regular and professional use of the theatre as a means of political education.

Gonne. By the same token, in the text, realistic prose dialogue is alternated with formal iambic verse, and also with a brand of informal 'sprung-rhythm' verse with rhyme, assonance and alliteration, carrying great variation in the length of line. This was intended as a vehicle for rapid vernacular speech, where verse was judged necessary because of the conventionality of the stage-business (i.e. passages of a few minutes which in fact summarised long historical periods of argument or travel between two locations), and where too much 'correctness' in the prosody would detract from the down-to-earth approach of the characters. For instance:

Connolly in Part Three explains his doubts about the potential of the Dublin Socialist Club, which has invited him to be its paid political organiser:

'The first remark I have to make
Brings a blush into my cheek:
But had we not best start as we mean to go on –
What sort of wage can I expect to earn?
The fact is, I can't imagine –
However large your subscription –
This club is in any way capable
Of employing a full-time official?
To do what work,
For how many days each week?
What facilities, what expenses, and basically for what hope?
This is a matter before which nothing else can be disposed:
As you know, I have a family to feed and house and clothe.'

The whole cycle is written to be accompanied by music, not alone where there are specified songs in the script, but as a background to certain speeches, and a punctuation to stage-movement and points of spoken argument. The settings are not particularised, except for certain placards with titles, or banners with slogans, at the back of the stage, and some stylised backcloths with emblematic pictures suggestive of the period – e.g. in Part Five: the gables of the little streets of Belfast with their opposed slogans (Loyalist/Protestant *v.* Nationalist/Catholic) under a massive outspread Red Hand of Ulster filling the sky; this emblem remains through all the Belfast sequences in this section. The plays are to be moved as fast as possible across a largely unfurnished stage, which ideally should extend in and among the audience, along gangways and platforms at different levels: though in practice at Liberty Hall we had to confine ourselves to a projecting apron-stage between two balcony-stages, and the fullest use we could make of the access-aisles of the auditorium.

Although it would be nice to be able to assure readers that nothing had gone into the plays which was not factually 'true', there are inevitably certain areas of the script where detailed accuracy had to be sacrificed in favour of *essential* (or *emblematic*) *truth*. This is not an evasion of responsibility: it is rather an acceptance that the responsibility of the playwright is not the same as that of the historian. In order, for instance, to clarify the complication of the story for an audience which must be assumed not to be expert in it, we found ourselves altering the date of young soldier Connolly's first arrival in Ireland (Part One) to coincide with the Phoenix Park Murders, whereas (according to Greaves) the murders had already taken place, and may well have been the reason for the regiment's Irish posting. Similarly we pretended in Part Three that Keir Hardie was an MP during the Boer War; in fact he had lost his seat in 1895. And when Jaurès is assassinated in 1914, we give Connolly a brief epitaph for him:

'All hail to at least one Continental Comrade who showed mankind that men still know how to die for the holiest of all causes, the sanctity of the human soul, the practical brotherhood of the human race . . .'

These words *were* written by Connolly in 1914, but alluded to a mistaken report of the death of *Liebknecht*. Also, while a fair proportion of Connolly's other speeches in the plays are direct quotes from his writings, we always held ourselves free to alter the syntax, run passages from different essays together, and combine them with lines of our own composition, provided such liberties would add to the *dramatic* effectiveness of the quotations in the context of the stage-action, and provided their *original* meaning was not thereby distorted. We would justify our conduct by pointing, say, to Shakespeare's *Julius Caesar*: after the death of Caesar and before the arrangements of reprisals by Antony, Octavius and Lepidus, there was in fact a lengthy episode of civil war between Octavius and Antony. But Shakespeare lets his audience imagine that the avengers of Caesar came together in reasonable amity without any delay. If he had kept to the actual historical facts, he would have muffled the main point of the second half of the play, which is of course the destruction of Brutus and Cassius and their cause at Philippi. The tension between Octavius and Antony can be perfectly well *suggested* by the way they discuss their proscriptions: and the story as a whole is clarified by the economy.

## Results of the Irish production

Our financial and administrative arrangements for *The Non-Stop Connolly Show* were as hand-to-mouth and ad hoc as such things always are in Dublin; and we were gratified to discover that the interest aroused by the plays was too great for our resources – many individuals and groups asked us to bring the show to their neighbourhoods and we were compelled to refuse them because we simply did not have the company any longer available. It was obvious that there is in fact a vast untapped demand for this sort of theatre in Ireland. As it was, on the few touring dates we did fulfill, we found that the very improvised nature of the production – few properties, no scenery, not always a full cast, and decisions having to be made at the very last moment about which scenes we could perform and with how many people, and whether or no we used a stage or did them in the centre of the audience – seemed to have added to the attraction of the work. It certainly gave people a feeling that the presentation of plays with some solidity of content was perfectly possible without having to accept all the normal apparatus of 'production-technique': and that fairly spontaneous street or yard performances could be a regular feature of Irish urban life.

We have been told that at least one political theatre group is now operating in a Catholic working-class area of Belfast. The Workers' Cultural Group in Dublin is contemplating taking a new play (specially commissioned) to a festival in Cuba in a year or two. The 'fringe theatre' in Dublin is expanding in many different directions with much greater flexibility of approach than hitherto – Jim Sheridan is now taking plays round the streets in a manner pioneered by the Connolly show in 1975. A politico-social Theatre Workshop is operating in Galway and has already done one street-play about a current industrial dispute and another indoor piece about the role of the university academic employee in a trade-union.

The press response on the whole was good. The reviewers in the national newspapers were not uniformly favourable – though one or two of them were very enthusiastic – but they all recognised the unique nature of the experiment and wrote about it accordingly. The regular 'establishment' of the Dublin theatre was not interested. They seem to have regarded us at worst as a threat to their *status quo*, and at best as a group of inconsiderable eccentrics who ought not to be indulged. There was, for example, no approach to us from the Abbey management, who might possibly have been expected to ask at least to look at a script . . .

In 1976 we were enabled to present the cycle as a series of 're-hearsed readings' – fifty minutes at a time, during lunch-hour – at the little Almost Free Theatre in Soho, London, run by a (recently naturalised) American, Ed Berman. Here we aroused a great deal of interest among certain areas of the acting profession, and the 'spontaneous' style of presentation seems to have attracted actors who came prepared to read parts without more than an hour or two of rehearsal and without getting paid for it. (There was a 'nucleus' permanent cast who were receiving the normal lunch-time-theatre wages.) This consecutive run of readings covered the whole cycle twice in five weeks. We had feared, and indeed had been warned, that interest in plays on Ireland in London was nil, and that we would get no audiences for so *outré* a project. But in the event we found that (except for one week or so in the middle, when our advertisement by an oversight had failed to appear in *Time Out*, and the weather was appallingly hot) the house was full for nearly every session. Several members of the audience actually succeeded in attending every section of the cycle.

At the same time, no interest was taken by the 'established' sub-sidised theatres. A National Theatre 'dramaturg' came twice, and did ask to read the script. He admitted that he knew nothing of the Irish situation, but said that if the National were to think of present-ing the cycle – and who else in London would have the resources for a full production? – they would find all their organisation thrown out of gear for four months: such a production would be out of the question. Our agent, having told us that the plays were utterly 'unsaleable', also saw two of them. In contrast to Dublin, the press virtually ignored us. Some reviewers came to one performance and wrote about it as though it had been the complete cycle. That the very fact of there being a 'complete cycle' was some sort of possibly important innovation did not appear to have struck them. Several of the newspapers sent no one to any of the performances. As far as we remember, the man from *The Times* was the only reviewer actu-ally to witness a number of the episodes. He saw six out of fourteen and then criticised the entire cycle, *as* a cycle, on the basis of less than half of it; which was a mixed blessing, as he inevitably missed the structural development of the story. On the other hand, there was real appreciation of our work from left-wing papers, notably *The Morning Star* and *The News Line*, which both published in-terviews with the authors. These journals are read by Socialists out-side Britain, so their coverage of the show did result in some over-seas interest.

Now was this 'edging away from the hem of our garments' by denizens of the 'regular channels' a deliberate boycott or was it merely accidental? Probably it was a bit of both. A large series of epic plays is in itself something that critics may not care to know about, because it is very difficult to assess, and they would all no doubt prefer to wait until it becomes as well known as Oberam-mergau before they try to evaluate it. (But if it is not reviewed with a proper appreciation of its intentions, how can it ever become a well-known as Oberammergau . . .?) Moreover, a large series of epic plays upon so 'controversial' and 'remote' a subject as the Irish Question becomes even more delicate a matter for 'evaluation'. Who knows, the reviewer or the prospective producer may find himself having to take sides upon something which may conceivably touch up against the Prevention of Terrorism Act . . . In Dublin, of course, there is the Offences Against the State Act. But this is not (as we have already shown – see p. 119 ff.) a product of consensus politics. And although our play did not 'incite acts of violence', it was certainly intended to gather together in Liberty Hall a congregation of protest against the current Fine Gael/Labour 'revision of history' attitudes, which deprecate the 1916 Rising on specious grounds, and are directly aimed at divorcing the idea of Republicanism from that of Socialism. (Apropos, a section of Part Three was shown as part of our publicity on an arts programme put out by the Dublin television station. A complete speech by Connolly was recorded: all of it was transmitted except for the final lines:

'Who dares to stand and tell me that Republicanism and Socialism are in no way compatible!
  In the academic exactitude of this funereal reading-room
  The lie has been refuted: the truth at last comes home!'

No doubt the speech *was* fifteen seconds too long for the available spot in the programme, and the producer found it easiest to cut it from the bottom? The rest of the speech had dealt with the nineteenth-century land agitation: a problem more or less solved by 1903 . . .)

But if there *was* an element of deliberate boycott of the work in London, we need look no further than the Labour Party Conference at Blackpool in 1976 to understand how it could come about. To quote from *The Irish Times* of 1 October 1976:

'The moment the very name of Ireland is mentioned, the English seem to bid adieu to common feeling, common prudence, and common sense.' This observation by Sydney Smith . . . might

well be applied to today's scheduled debate on Northern Ireland
at the Labour Party Conference . . .

We witnessed the debate on television: the arguments for and
against the removal of troops from the province were appalling in
their ineptitude; and the motion itself was so combined with other
incompatible resolutions that one could only conclude there was
behind it some crafty determination to mislead the delegates. No
understanding was allowed to be conveyed of the real reasons for the
warfare in Ulster, no relation of the political situation there to that
in Britain (except for the vaguely ominous 'If civil war breaks out
there, it's going to spill over into this country' – but how, and between which factions, of course, left quite unstated), and above all
no feeling that the streets of Belfast are perhaps a little nearer
Blackpool than those of Timbuctoo. The Irish Question – in short –
was handled as though it were a bomb which might go off unless
it was held absolutely at arm's length, and tossed out of window
before anyone had a chance to *examine it at all closely.*

A series of plays about Connolly is either of no value to anyone,
or else it is precisely that *close examination* of the entire Irish problem which the Labour Party platform refused to permit at Blackpool. One aspect of the history, for example, which was never discussed in the Conference, and which stood out like a malign light-
house from the rocks and reefs of our dramatised complexities, is
the role of the Conservative Party, allied with the Army General
Staff, allied with the Ulster Unionists, and the way in which this
unholy grouping has systematically – from the nineteenth century
on – used Ireland to defeat Labour in Britain and used Labour in
Britain to defeat the Irish. Anyone who can grasp what General
Wilson and Carson were up to in 1914 can also understand why
Harold Wilson and Merlyn Rees were unable to use soldiers to
break the strike of the Loyalist Workers in 1974 which in turn
broke the 'power-sharing' Assembly. On the stage, in a succession
of short scenes in rapid juxtaposition, a figure of a red-coated, fierce-
masked General (loosely referred to as 'General Wilson', but in
fact representing a whole body of such types) can be shown domin-

ating the dramatic action over a period of years; and thereby a point is *graphically* established that would take ages to lay out in the narrative of a political speech.

It is precisely this kind of 'elucidatory exposition' which we believe to be the main contribution of politico-historical theatre to contemporary public affairs. It is not so much 'propagandist' as exploratory and educational. But it *is* propagandist in that it finally brings the authors, and consequently the audience, to some 'partisan' conclusion. All conclusions about the state of contemporary affairs must inevitably be partisan – as we have stated, consensus is not possible in a divided society – and the real issue here is 'can the point of view of the play be justified when the actions illustrating it are presented on stage in public, and held up to the judgement of an audience?'

If the members of the Labour Movement in Britain cannot at last lay hold of the connection between the imperial legacy of Ireland and the failure of the working class to secure control of the British economy, they will never be able to solve either of these crucial problems. Let us conclude with a quotation from a recent article in the Irish *Sunday Press* (10 October 1976) by Proinsias Mac Aonghusa – whose original Connolly anthology got us working on the plays in the first place. This left-wing commentator writes, as an Irishman looking at the British Labour and Conservative annual Conferences:

> Neither party had anything worthwhile to say about their interferences in Ireland: but, at least, Tory speakers knew facts and spoke with some authority, while at the Labour Conference both those who favoured a Black-and-Tan solution in Ireland and those who supported in some measure Irish national aspirations spoke from deep ignorance of the facts.
>
> It is right to record that the Labour Conference voted against the proposition that Ireland should be independent and socialist. Had the talk been about some far-off Asian land, doubtless the calls for independence and socialism would raise the roof.
>
> Ireland's failure to break with sterling in 1933, and again in 1949, now places us in England's sinking ship. It is therefore in

our interests to have a government in London which might be trusted by the money men. On the evidence of Blackpool and Brighton that would likely be a Tory Government ...

For an Irish Socialist to advocate Tory rule in England is of course the utter negation of all that Connolly stood for:* and we have no doubt Mr Mac Aonghusa is well aware of this. It is up to the British 'Left' to prove his diagnosis mistaken. The refusal of London theatre critics and managements to treat plays seriously that deal with Irish historical themes is but one small symptom of the imperial arrogance reflected much more strongly on the wider political scene. As our 'fictional' Connolly and Larkin say to one another at the end of Part Five, when their General Strike has collapsed, and the TUC have rejected their pleas for support:

CONNOLLY: They grunt and shout against us and they yell
    Like wolves and badgers of the dark wild wood –
LARKIN: No, rabbits, lurking in their safe protective hole.
CONNOLLY: We Irish workers once more go down to hell –
    We eat no bread of common sacrifice and brotherhood
    But choke our tongues with dust of black betrayal.
    Dublin, defeated, now is left alone.
LARKIN: Can we continue all upon our own?
CONNOLLY: The red flag of the peoples of the world
    Has no room in it for a single patch of green ...?

* Though there was one occasion, during the great lockout, when Connolly did appeal to his working-class supporters in Britain to vote against the Asquith Liberals during the bye-elections if the London Government continued to ignore the plight of Dublin. Labour at this time was largely aligned with the Liberals in Parliament. The vote that Connolly called for would have been much to the advantage of the Tories.

The text of *The Non-Stop Connolly Show* is shortly to be published by Pluto Press.

# The Chhau Dancers of Purulia

## 1971

Purulia is a barren and hilly district of West Bengal lying towards the west at the border of Bihar. It is covered at places by dense forests leaving small pockets here and there for agriculture. Rainfall is inadequate and life is extremely difficult. The people who live there are mostly aboriginals and semi-aboriginals: they speak a western dialect of Bengali, generally known as Kurmali: as the people are known as Kurmis. Among this people there is prevalent a form of dance known as the Chhau dance ... ritualistic in character, and performed ceremonially during the last days of the Bengali year on the occasion of the annual worship of the popular Sun-God ... Every performance starts with the invocation of Ganesha ...

*From an informatory leaflet published by the*
*West Bengal Research Institute of Folk-Culture.*

The village was unreachable by an ordinary car – our Land-Rover, on leaving the main road, was directed over a mile or two of terraced rice-fields in the dark, the only indication of the route being the tracks across the dry fallow ground made by the villagers' bullock-carts. At every division between the fields the vehicle bumped and lurched alarmingly over the earthen bank built to retain the irrigation water which fills the fields when the crop is growing. The village loomed up in front of us – there were of course no lights showing, and the mud walls of the thatched cottages were much the same colour as the night. We realised we were there because the white cotton clothes of the villagers who came to meet us suddenly stood out in the headlights like luminous traffic signs on a Western highway. The faces of the people were not visible – being aboriginals, they are much darker than the ordinary caste-Hindu, a quasi-Negroid type, short in stature and of a precise neatness in figure and movement. There seemed to be thousands and thousands of them. An Indian village looks, architecturally, to be about the same size as an English settlement of – say – two thousand people, but there may be five times that number of persons clustered into the poky habitations. Seventeen enthusiastic young men raced and leaped about in front of the Landrover, waving their arms at us like demented traffic cops, directing the driver – in apparent defiance of all common sense – into the 'main street'. This was an alley about four inches wider than the car. The eaves of the cottages were brushed by the luggage rack, the mudguards threatened at every moment to take entire walls away. Women and children pressed themselves into the four inches, more concerned to see the car come past than to attempt to get out of its way. Moth-eaten village dogs sprang in rage against the wheels. No one was run over, no house was demolished. We parked in a sort of cul-de-sac from which there seemed no possibility of ever getting out again.

The dances were to be performed in a section of the main street which was slightly wider than the rest. An area perhaps twenty by thirty feet was kept clear by serious older men armed with thick bamboo cudgels. At intervals they aimed blows at the naked children who constantly endeavoured to encroach upon this level rectangle, though I never actually saw any of the children hit. It was rather a melodramatic demonstration that a formal occasion was taking place. The village elders sat on a row of kitchen chairs – about twelve chairs altogether. These old men had the appearance of those Roman senators who sat in their chairs waiting for the irruption of the wild Gauls into the Forum. They leaned severely upon their bamboo staves, puffed slowly at their brown 'beedi' cigarettes, frowned at the children and discussed matters obviously of grave moment – much nodding of grey heads and pursing of magisterial mouths. The rest of the male population crowded around excitedly, pushing, scrimmaging, laughing and joking. Something like an English football crowd before the match begins. All around the dancing area grandstands had been erected, consisting of string beds lashed at various levels to scaffold poles. They were swaying and tottering under the weight of hundreds of women and children – the women still sat on the sagging bed frames, their legs crossed, but their apparent repose was contradicted by the continual twisting of their torsos as they turned their heads now here, now there, to yell good-humoured badinage at their friends and relations across the way. (Aboriginal and semi-aboriginal women have none of the gazelle-like decorum of the high-caste Hindu ladies whom we are used to in the West – the older ones resemble Mother Courage, the younger ones Polly Garter.) The children screamed and plunged and dangled their legs over thin air – babies on scaffold poles balanced themselves like monkeys. None of them fell off.

We were shown up a vertical ladder onto one of the grandstands. I had been ill and soon began to feel very dizzy. I came down again. One of the elders offered me a chair. I felt an impostor, sitting there among the councilmen. It was a tribute to my white skin I could well have done without; but in fact the embarrassment was needless – in five minutes I was forgotten, except by the very busy youths who kept pressing glasses of tea into my fist and offering me beedis. The whole village was alive with hospitality and excitement. The roar of drums announced the arrival of the dancers – they had walked from their own village about thirty miles away and before entering they formed up in a precisely ordered procession, their masks and costumes carried like a king's crown in a Shakespeare play, with ritualistic grandeur, the drummers leading the column whacking their great drums in a violent military rhythm: Tum-ti-ti tum-tum tum-TUM, tum-ti-ti tum-tum tum-TUM! As soon as they came into the dancing area they were absorbed by the crowd and disappeared into a back corner where they had to put on their costumes and where they were also served with glasses of tea and so on. It was now about nine o'clock at night. There were half a dozen high-power kerosene lamps hung on posts around the dancing area – all else was pitch darkness. We waited and waited. The arrival of the dancers was not, it seemed, a sign that the performance was just about to begin. I noticed a row of children sitting very high up on the very edge of the roof of the village post office, their average age perhaps two and a half. None of them fell off.

The dancers were all male, most of them young, some of them children.

About midnight the drummers came into the dancing area and began to play. Two of them manhandled enormous kettledrums about three feet in diameter. Three of them carried small cylindrical drums which were slung by cords from their necks and beaten at both ends. One musician played a wind instrument a little like an oboe – it made a high wailing noise, a bagpipe sort of noise. The kettledrums were placed on the ground and beaten with thick billets of wood. The cylinder-drummers stalked about the dancing area, up and down and round and round, playing a quicker and lighter rhythm as against the kettledrummers' Prussian thunder. The oboe-man writhed and swayed like the line of his own melody. A saturnine fellow with long greasy hair and a Zapata moustache came into the middle of the dancing area and casually began to sing, not very loudly (and the audience didn't mind, they went on chattering and laughing full-pitch) but with the enormous melodramatic gestures of an old-fashioned Neapolitan tenor – yet the gestures, like his singing, were oddly thrown away. Then he withdrew, as casually as he had come. The drummers changed their rhythm, it became faster, more exciting, the cylinder-drummers moved towards the entry left among the audience at one corner of the dancing area, their eyes glaring into the darkness outside as they played; then they moved back again, then forward, as though conjuring someone or something into the arena – a conjuration that would only work if they sweated for it long enough. Their movements behind their drums became a furious dance, they did indeed sweat, their bare feet pounded the dust, their fingers on the drumskins moved so fast one could hardly see them move. Then suddenly, from out of the darkness, gleaming and jingling in white and silver and black, Ganesha was made manifest.

Ganesha is a god with an elephant-head. As danced in the Chhau he is a small boy wearing a suit of black jacket and trousers, all spangled with sequins and embroidery; bare feet, bells around his ankles, and a huge mask entirely covering his head and shoulders. A cheekily tilted trunk about eighteen inches long. A crown of coloured beadwork nodding above his white brow. He walked into the arena very slowly, pacing like a toy soldier. There was nothing human about him at all. He was – to an audience already prepared by deep belief and the music of the drums – an incarnate deity who was gracing their village by his presence. It was as though there had been a fair chance that he might never turn up at all, it seemed of no importance that everyone had observed the boy who danced him walk into the street three hours earlier carrying the mask and then drink a glass of tea before getting into his costume. For the first time I really understood what Greek tragedy must have been like in the days of Thespis, when it was ceasing to be a rural ritual and was moving into the new city theatres. The 'purpose of theatre' – a vague concept continually argued about in our professional Western journals – was entirely clear in this context. The purpose of theatre was to bring the gods down to earth for the space of a few hours in order to secure the continuance of life for mankind. Ganesha strutted, he threw out his little brown feet, he tinkled and jingled and some of his movements made me laugh. They made the villagers laugh too – Ganesha in the legends is a mischievous little fellow, the favourite child of his divine parents, easily frightened by malevolent deities but on occasion sturdy and surprisingly brave. Then, one by one, came in the other characters in the fable. I don't know who they all were – strange creatures with twelve arms and blue or green masks, all human in shape, except for Ganesha, but with an aloof sardonic humanity like Greek archaic sculpture – cold superior smiles and raised eyebrows. The female masks of the goddesses were much like the male ones, distinguished only by the absence of moustaches. The masks were crowned with great erections of beads and wirework, making the (normally undersized) Kurmi peasants into awe-inspiring giants.

Some of the characters were demons with tusks instead of teeth, and ferocious whiskers. One dancer played a peacock-character, with a white human mask, a peacock head and neck protruding from around his waist, and a practicable tail which opened and shut splendidly, made of real peacock's feathers. Most of the costumes were like Ganesha's – black suits with spangles. Demons were more or less naked with streaks of blue body-paint. Goddesses wore elaborate coloured saris. All had bare feet and ankle-bells. Most of the male characters (and some female) carried weapons – swords, bows-and-arrows, spears – all decorated with coloured ribbons and tinsel. The great goddess Kali – mother and destroyer – wore a black jumper, a miniskirt, a necklace of human skulls, a long wild-haired wig, and her red mouth was contorted into a wide snarl, her tongue stuck out between her teeth. Her mask was black. She looked like a girl from Harlem who had emigrated to the East Village and joined a revolutionary commune. She was very danger-ous and stamped on the men whom she killed. She had a curious twentieth-century Western sexuality – perhaps because (being danced by a man) her chest was flat beneath her jumper and her hips and legs were slender. (This raises a lot of odd sexual-sociological questions I haven't time to go into here.)

Before they were compelled by outside forces to become farmers and grow rice (in a most unsuitable climate), the Kurmis were hunters in the forest and warriors. All the dances performed in the Chhau festival are short dramatisations of episodes from Hindu mythology which deal in some way with fighting or hunting. The steps of the dances are the steps of war dances or the movements of huntsmen stalking their prey or the movements of the animals they used to catch. If they tried to hunt nowadays they would probably get into trouble with the Forest Department of the government and its constables. It is a safe bet in India that any aboriginal people are liable to be in trouble with the forest constables. The dances went on all night until dawn broke. I fell asleep at one point and dreamed dreams of battles and murders to the rhythms of the drums. At intervals I half-woke and saw through bleary eyes the same con-tinuous stamping up and down of proud spangled giants, waving their spears and threatening each other with their arrows. From beginning to end the noise was enormous. I was not the only person in the audience who fell asleep – it did not seem to matter. The gods were there and their power was in the village, whether the people slept or woke. They had been called up and they had arrived.

I have tried to present above an immediate and subjective view of the Chhau dances as seen, more or less unprepared, by a European visitor. The rest of this essay, I hope, will eschew prose-poetry and will put forward a few facts. The Chhau dances were discovered only a few years ago by Professor Bhattacharyya of the West Bengal Institute of Folk-Culture. There are many backwoods areas of India even today where all sorts of folk-dances and dramas may be going on quite unknown to the outside world, and the various official and semi-official institutes of folk culture are engaged in research programmes – ill-financed and undermanned – to bring them to the notice of the aforesaid outside world. The history of the Chhau dance is not quite clear, but apparently something over a century ago the Kurmi people were converted to Hinduism by decree of their chief – who no doubt wanted more of a part in 'the making of modern India'. Before this time the religion of these tribesmen had been animistic and very primitive. In order to establish the new religion in depth, the ruler had the traditional war and hunting dances modified so that they came to illustrate the traditional mythology of the Hindus, which is similar in many ways to that of the ancient Greeks of about the time of Plato; i.e. for the peasants there is a collection of poetically conceived gods and goddesses, while for the upper intellectual castes a whole range of ethical and philosophical thought is built upon (but never quite hides from sight) the basic polytheistic structure. The comparison with the Greeks should not, however, be carried too far. Sophocles added to and altered the material of Aeschylus, as Aeschylus had done to the material of Homer, and as Euripides was to do to the material of Sophocles. In India the work of art, once established, becomes fixed; and the rules of dance and drama demand strict obedience to what has been done before. The quality of an artist is recognised in the skill with which he fulfils the traditional patterns, not in the originality with which he improves upon them. Whatever the Kurmis' dances were before the conversion, afterwards there can be no doubt that the form has been conservative in origin and intention.

Dr Bhattacharyya found the Chhau dances in a rather poor way. They were becoming neglected and in many villages only a remnant was left of what they once had been. Filled with enthusiasm for what he had discovered, the professor set about reviving the form. In order to do so, he instituted an annual competition. At a central point in the district of Purulia (a bungalow, in fact belonging to the Forest Department), he brought together the best troupes from many different villages and had them perform before an audience of specially invited people from all over India and other parts of the world. The best troupe was rewarded by being brought to New Delhi, where they were presented before the cosmopolitan society of the capital. As the dancers are not full-time professionals but peasants who dance in their own home-districts at a season when agriculture is unavoidably at a standstill, it is not surprising that this trip to the great city – for men who never else would have travelled beyond their own immediate confines – acted as an enormous incentive, and interest in the dances among the villages immediately began to grow. But why had it slackened in the first place? Because of the poverty of the area – one of the most backward in all that part of India. Is the poverty in any way alleviated by the revival of the Chhau? Not at all. Professor Bhattacharyya has no funds with which to subsidise the troupes – he himself is unsubsidised by the government, though he has been trying for years to obtain some sort of grant – and therefore any improvement in the costumes and general presentation of the dance must come out of the resources of the villagers.

The costumes and particularly the masks are extremely expensive. The masks are made of papier-mâché and crowned with their elaborate bead and wire work by the inhabitants of one village alone. These craftsmen do not dance, but at the season of the New Year everyone in that village works in some way to prepare the masks for all the dance troupes in the district. The village is the only village in the district which is inhabited exclusively by caste-Hindus. The Kurmis – as aboriginals – are presumably in some way 'untouchable' to caste-Hindus, though the whole caste-system is so complex (as well as being 'illegal', like racial discrimination in the United States) that I do not feel I can go any further into expounding it here – very few Indians seem to understand it themselves. At all events, the mask-makers belong to a more superior order in society than the dancers; and they charge a lot for their (admittedly exquisite) work. We were shown one mask that cost 600 rupees, whereas the average *yearly* income of the peasant is perhaps no more than 500 rupees. One troupe of dancers may perhaps require a dozen or more masks – though they will not all be so expensive as the prize example we saw. On the other hand, the masks have to be renewed every year – the dances are very violent and the masks get damaged fairly soon in the season. When the dancers fight, they do not merely 'mime' a combat – they mix in with each other tooth and nail like all-in wrestlers. It can easily be seen, then, that the equipment of a first-rate troupe will rapidly make a huge hole in the community exchequer. Dr Bhattacharyya told us of families who had gone bankrupt in order to make their troupe the best in the competition, and of one troupe-leader who had committed suicide as a result of the economic pressure.

When – after our visit to the dance in the village – we saw the official competition at the Forest Rest-House bungalow, we saw the same dances, but performed in a very different setting. The government Forest Department – which, as I have suggested, has a relationship with the peasants resembling that of the Sheriff of Nottingham with Robin Hood and his band – provided a dancing area of the usual shape and size, but surrounded by *barbed wire* (to prevent undesirable persons interfering – i.e. local peasants who came and watched the dance in addition to the regular invited guests like ourselves) and patrolled by the forest constables in police uniform, armed with loaded cudgels. At one point between the dances I saw these fellows beating up two men whom they thought were 'troublemakers' but who turned out to be the musicians for the next dance who had thoughtlessly climbed the fence in order to take their places during the interval. An ugly episode, no doubt embarrassing to the Professor, if he had noticed it, but the natural consequence of relying for administrative arrangements upon what one could not help thinking of as 'the pig power structure'.

Yet upon whom could Dr Bhattacharyya rely? Without the co-operation of the forest officers no one can do anything in those wild parts of the country. And he did manage to walk his narrow tightrope and keep reasonably good relationships with both the officials and the villagers. Indeed everyone seemed devoted to him – he himself was so genuinely devoted to the local people and their art.

Two of the naked demon-dancers, wrestling in their dance, threw each other against the barbed wire. One of them had a twelve-inch cut down his bare back. He danced on regardless, probably never noticed; but in that climate the wound might well have festered and become lethal in a day or two had he been unlucky.

In front of the government bungalow there could be no question of the gods visiting the village and blessing it. Government bunga-lows are not the normal haunts of errant deities. The dance simply became a performance – like *Peer Gynt* at Lincoln Centre.

The guests whom Dr Bhattacharyya had invited included two playwrights from Britain, a director from an experimental theatre in Denmark, a dance critic from a sophisticated Bombay journal, a lady from Paris representing UNESCO, and a professor from the drama department of a US university. All were well furnished with tape recorders, flash cameras and various other apparatus including copious notebooks. The US professor was the most egregious of our incongruous little group. He scrambled over the barbed wire (helped by the constable – my God, they didn't beat *him* up) and danced among the dancers, flashing his camera and sticking the mike of his tape recorder into the musicians' faces. If the dance was now *Peer Gynt* at Lincoln Centre, it was *Peer Gynt* at the press preview. Unsophisticated and illiterate those peasants may have been, but they knew a camera when they saw one.

Instead of dancing 'in the round' for the benefit of all the audience, they imperceptibly metamorphosed their act into a proscenium arch display, pointing everything at the academics – maybe they didn't even realise they were doing it. The academics recorded and re-corded. The archives will now be stuffed, the doctoral theses already lying on the publishers' shelves.

How much do Western professors pay impoverished Indian villagers to perform their dances for the benefit of the university archives? Nothing. The men who came to the Forest Rest-House had walked anything up to fifty miles lugging their gear in the hot sun. They danced all night and then walked home again the next day. They were not fed. Dr Bhattacharyya had no funds to buy food for them all – there must have been a few hundred altogether. The visitors did not expect to be asked to pay, so they (we) had brought no spare cash. Not wise to travel in India with wads of money – there are a lot of thieves about . . . An American professor on an archival jaunt among the West Bengal foothills is usually operating on some form of foundation grant. This will not be un-generous, because American enterprise in the subcontinent has accumulated many rupees which the Indian currency regulations do not permit to be exported, and so – by the serpentine dealings of international dollar-finance – the money is waiting in Indian banks for someone like a professor from Idaho to come along and spend it upon work of cultural benefit. Benefit to whom? No one in the States performs Chhau dances. If choreographers or dancers wish to understand the Chhau – in its entirety – they can only do so by witnessing it (as we were fortunate enough to do) in the centre of a populated village, among the people for whom it was intended and for whom the annual visit of the gods is an urgent necessity.

The whole scene was one of cultural exploitation following close upon the heels of material ditto. India – as everyone knows – is in a bad way economically. The rich half of the world has drained that country dry and is now dumping rubbish therein (I mean fertilisers that have been long disused in the West because of their polluting qualities; I mean third-rate textbooks on agriculture that no US-based agronomist would dream of keeping on his shelves;

I mean tractors for the 'green revolution' that arrive with no spare parts, break down in the fields; and then remain there for ever rusting while the farmers wearily yoke up their old bullock-teams once again). This rubbish is called 'Aid to Developing Nations' and is given – by the USA, the UK, the USSR – mainly because they want to keep the Chinese out.

Now there is in India a growing number of people who urgently would like to get the Chinese *in*. Not as conquerors, but as assistants and inspirers in that Indian peasant revolution that has never yet arrived, but which will inexorably have to come. It is already beginning in certain areas, notably in parts of West Bengal. Not in the district of Purulia – yet. It seems to me that – as a necessary preliminary to such revolution is the weakening of the bonds of traditional religion – the very business of taking a moribund religious art form and reviving it in the guise of *'Peer Gynt* at Lincoln Centre' may go far to bringing Purulia into the Maoist handclasp. I don't know. But if I were a Marxist-Leninist rural agitator – such people are often to be found under the outward appearance of the local schoolmaster or stationmaster or even forest officer – I would seriously consider making use of the technical excellence of the Chhau dancers and deftly persuading the artists to vary the content into a more revolutionary channel. It is not as difficult as it sounds. The old tribal dances were not long since varied to suit Hindu purposes. But that variation was imposed upon the people from above. The new thing is to get the people to impose their own variations from *inside*. The point is that Dr Bhattacharyya's festival has both secularised the dance – *to a certain extent* – and given the people a glimpse of better things – only a week's visit to New Delhi, it is true, but in so stagnant and apathetic a society, such brief experiences can sometimes be explosive. I may say that Dr Bhattacharyya very much disapproves of mixing art with politics and he does not like Marxist-Leninism. But his actions may have consequences that he has not quite foreseen.

The precise recording and archiving of the dance by foreign academics I hold to be dangerous nonsense. I know that many people will hold what I hold to be dangerous nonsense. But I hope that this essay will perhaps have brought out – even if only tentatively – some of the many contradictions inherent in the whole business of reviving and studying folk drama in backward cultural areas in the Third World.

One final contradiction. About a month after our visit to Purulia, we read in a Calcutta paper that the rains had failed there and scores of people – hundreds, was it? I forget – had perished in the drought and the consequent famine. It happens every year in one corner or the other of India. But I wondered how many of those enthusiastic young men who had pressed glasses of tea upon me when I sat absurdly on a hard chair among their village elders are now dead. How many of the reverend elders, how many of their women and children who had chattered away like starlings on the scaffolds? And will this be recorded in the university archives, and if so, who will read it? Mrs Gandhi was sufficiently alarmed by the situation to make a personal visit to Purulia. She was stoned by the crowd – by a right-wing element among the crowd, oddly enough. She appealed to the left-wing element to support her and the left-wing element thereupon stoned the right-wing element. Something is moving at all events, in the 'barren and hilly district'.

*Footnote on poverty:*
It may well be asked, 'If the peasants are so poor, how is it that they can ever have afforded to do these expensive dances at all?' The answer in many cases is that the village troupes have been subsidised by the local landlords. These landlords are caste-Hindus and desirous of preserving traditional religious forms (such as the Chhau) in order to preserve the Kurmis in their traditional *social* place – i.e. down at the bottom, where they own no land and are, as like as not, paid for their work on the landlords' fields in rice, of which they eat a proportion and then have to sell the rest in order to get that money which they need in order to buy the other, non-edible necessities of life. One dancer told us that he was not particularly enamoured of dancing – it is very hard work, after all – but when there is no work in the fields it is better to dance than do nothing. Besides, the troupes *are* given refreshments of a sort in

the villages where they perform.

The landlords, who are caste-Hindus, are also – with their dependent henchmen and servants – the 'right-wing element' which threw stones at Mrs Gandhi. It is of course impossible for a foreigner to find out exactly what is going on in the extremely complicated society of India. It is only obvious that whatever is going on, there is always something nasty at the root of it somewhere; and any attempt at examining any particular social set-up in detail has to be pursued like a detective story – look for clues to lead you to the villain. It is a fairly safe bet that the villain is *not* the most unlikely suspect, but the most likely – the landlord. Behind the landlord, often at a considerable distance, looms the shadowy figure of the 'next most likely suspect' – the United States of America. As a left-wing English writer, I am – in the Third World context – naturally regarded as an active agent of the United States of America. Why? Because I arrived in India in a car and am well fed. I know no way of avoiding this suspicion. An Indian Marxist-Leninist who may chance upon this article *in an American magazine* would be pardoned for thinking that it was in some mysteriously sophisticated way yet another weapon directed against him, instead of what it is meant to be: a piece of direct propaganda on his behalf.

Part Four

*The Matter of Britain*

A curious circumstance about the content of my plays – years after they have been written and performed, events have as it were come full circle, I find my imaginative figments turning out as established fact, by no means invariably to my satisfaction. *Serjeant Musgrave's Dance* (1959) dealt with a massacre of civilians during a British Army colonial 'peace-keeping' operation at the same time as a bitter colliery strike in England. In January 1972 thirteen people were shot dead by the Paras in Derry, while industrial trouble raged in the coalfields on a level unknown since the 1920s. While this was happening, I was at work with D'Arcy on an early draft of *The Non-Stop Connolly Show*: in a sense the whole story of Connolly was a kind of inside-out version of my invented Black Jack Musgrave. The latter was an old soldier who, sickened of the oppressive role of the Army in the colonies, deserts, and attempts to strike a blow against his masters: by his inability to understand the political implications of the labour movement (the striking pitmen), he fails, and is executed. Connolly, as a young soldier, follows the colours in Ireland, is repelled by his cruel duties, deserts, and then devotes the rest of his life to forging such links between Irish Nationalism and International Labour as surely would not fail when put to the test. But the inability of British Labour to understand the political implications of Irish Separatism brings about the isolation of the 1916 Dublin Rising, and Connolly is captured and executed by his sometime comrades of the British Army . . .

*The Royal Pardon* (written with D'Arcy in 1966) shows a theatre company which makes a mess of a play about King Arthur and

Merlin: their show is saved by a stage-hand and an actress, who are treated like dogs by the manager, are vindictively hounded by an officer of the law, and are eventually left to pursue their own theatrical destinies while the company complacently receives the honour of appointment to the Royal Household with munificent subsidy. The next essay in this book gives as objective a view as possible of the disagreement between myself and D'Arcy (as co-authors of *The Island of the Mighty*) on one hand, and the Royal Shakespeare Company on the other, in 1972. The conclusion we drew from this parlous affair was that all playwrights in Britain should, as a matter of urgency, organise themselves into some sort of Union to protect their artistic as well as their financial interests – a point also developed in the last essay of this book.

Such an organisation is, at the time of writing, indeed in process of establishing itself.* It is called The Theatre Writers' Union, and has already proved itself well aware of the problems to be faced and the political difficulties that lie in the way of their solution. Time will show whether enough professional solidarity can be maintained to make this Group into a truly effective agent of change. There is really no good reason why not ...

At such meetings of the TWU as I have been able to attend the most fervent discussion has been on the subject of censorship. The abolition of the Lord Chamberlain's function in this regard has by no means resulted in a Theatre of Free Speech, let alone Free Opinion.

In 1964 I dedicated my *Armstrong's Last Goodnight* to Conor Cruise O'Brien, upon whose Congo memoirs I had founded a good deal of the narrative. Shortly afterwards he took a leading part in exposing the way the CIA penetrated allegedly independent cultural and educational foundations and subverted them in the interests of US State Department policy. As an Irish politician he has actively supported the retention of the British armed forces in Northern Ireland. Part of the work of the British armed forces has been the setting-up of a singular activity known as Psyops, whereby – according to documents published in *The Irish Times* – civil servants from Whitehall have been trained by the *military* in such matter as 'gathering and supplying propaganda material for radio, television, newspapers, and magazines' ... as part of 'planned

* see page 158, (Late Footnote).

psychological activities in peace and war ... in order to create attitudes and behaviour favourable to the achievement of political and military objectives'.

Exactly which civil servants have attended these interesting courses, and what precise work they have been assigned upon graduation, has not been vouchsafed – even in answer to questions put down in the House of Commons. The courses began in 1972. About that time the ability of the theatre or the radio/TV media to present serious dramatic studies of, for example, the Irish situation, began to be observably and consistently interfered with. I am by no means the only dramatist to have come up against a block on this particular highway. But if one is convinced, as I am, that Northern Ireland is Britain's Vietnam, and if the Psyops project is as closely-related to CIA technique as it appears to be, then surely it is not a symptom of acute paranoia to believe that the drama (at some remote area of decision-making) has been marked down for observation, and, if necessary, remote control. Remote control, after all, requires no formal censorship: merely, as has always been the traditional British way, a Word in the Right Place ... The Right Place will usually be the administrators of the public funds, wherever these are devoted to the 'encouragement of the arts'.

The great difficulty is that dramatists will rarely be told: 'Your play is *subversive*: we are imposing a political restriction upon its performance': an aesthetic or bureaucratic reason will rather be advanced. The play is too long; the cast is too large; the project does not qualify for a grant because of some unfortunate technicality, perhaps the author's normal residence is outside the UK ... and so on. In my case it has been incontrovertibly passed on to me (though never put down on paper in so many words) that any work of mine done in collaboration with D'Arcy (which in effect means all my Irish material) is altogether out of line with the requirements of more than one subsidised theatre: the nearest anyone came to expressing this loud and clear was a communication to my agent, from a lucrative and normally liberal source of patronage, that a new play could be commissioned – provided that it was *a genuine Arden work*. As I have not been in the habit of palming off the work of others as my own, I could draw only the one inference.

It occurred to me later that there was possibly another way of interpreting the cryptic phrase: that 'a genuine Arden work' in fact meant 'a play like *Serjeant Musgrave's Dance*, which does not come to any very positive conclusion' – whereas *non-genuine Arden* would be 'Arden at last affirming from his own hard experience the need for revolution and a Socialistic society: and moreover convinced that his artistic independence and integrity will be strengthened rather than compromised by so *doctrinaire* a stance . . .'

Twelve years ago I looked on at people's struggles, and wrote about them for the stage, sympathetically, but as an onlooker. Without consciously intending it, I have become a participant. These essays I hope will show how. I write from henceforth in that capacity. It can't be helped.

*Late Footnote: May 1977:**
Since the above was written the Theatre Writers' Union has most definitely established itself, and has demanded recognition as a negotiating body from the National Theatre and the other big metropolitan subsidised theatres.

# Playwrights on Picket
(*Written in collaboration with Margaretta D'Arcy*)

## 1973

In the autumn of 1972 the Royal Shakespeare Company decided to present the three plays that make up *The Island of The Mighty* – or rather about 65 per cent of them – at the Aldwych Theatre, London. Though the trilogy was truncated it was still very long and rehearsals were scheduled to last eight weeks. A complete run-through of the entire piece did not take place until two weeks before the opening. After seeing the run-through, both authors realised that the overall balance of the production had shifted significantly. Also, the allowed running time was being exceeded to such an extent that radical cuts – about thirty minutes' worth of text – had to be made. It was difficult for the playwrights to know how these cuts should be selected, owing to the lack of balance in the presentation – not only in the acting but also in the music and the décor, which differed considerably in their effect from what had been promised by an earlier hearing of unorchestrated melodies and viewing of small-scale sketches and models.

The playwrights were under contract to attend rehearsals and do necessary work on the text, for which they were paid. Why were the actors in some scenes now playing their parts so strangely? Because they did not understand the play? Or had they been deliberately shifted from their original readings of the roles, to pursue some idea held by the director? The same questions applied to the music and the sets. The director had in fact spent the greater part of the week, before the run-through, working with the cast on his own. He explained that the presence of a playwright could act at times as a 'cop-out', or refuge, for an actor who was having difficulty with his part, and he therefore requested this seclusion. His wish was respected, but the results were disturbing to the authors. It was clear that their disappointment with the run-through was shared by at least some of the cast – several approached the writers the same evening and asked if they could persuade the director to call a general company meeting the next day to discuss thoroughly both the meaning and the interpretation of the play.

Only the playwright can understand the *meaning* of a new, unperformed play. He may not understand it all that well, but when it comes to improving defects in the structure, no one else can be certain what the structure is intended to express. The business of *interpretation* (i.e. *how* the meaning is presented on the stage) is the department of the director. The authors of *The Island* believed that only a complete analysis of both elements, carried out with the help of everyone concerned (i.e. director and actors as well as composer and scene-designers) would serve to get the play back on to the rails from which it seemed to have slipped so suddenly. But more than that: such an analysis would also establish which parts of the text were redundant to the *meaning* and which were distorted because of faulty *interpretation*. Until this was done no accurate abridgement was possible. When the authors explained this to the director, he replied that he feared such a meeting, at this point in rehearsal, might demoralise the actors. (He did not consider the possibility that, on the contrary, it could *lift* their morale.) He declared himself sure he knew what he was doing, and asked only to be let alone to complete the scheme of work he had laid out. He did not agree that the meaning of the play was becoming distorted. He attributed any unsatisfactory parts of the run-through to individual minor causes and felt that the whole work would shape up very well. The writers realised there was now a fundamental incompatibility between his ideas and theirs, and thought it best to go home to Ireland; the director agreed. But before they left London, they said they must have the meeting, and they would not go until it was held. They had still to make the text cuts and this important work must be properly prepared for. The director said he would arrange a meeting, not immediately, but later in the week. The following morning the writers contacted their agent, asking her to make sure the meeting was to be scheduled as soon as possible. When she communicated with the director, she discovered his attitude had hardened overnight: he now said that the meeting would serve no useful purpose and he would not allow it. The authors were thus faced with a one-sided repudiation of their contractual rights. They decided not to accept it passively and considered what to do.

The previous year the authors had joined the Society of Irish Playwrights, which is affiliated with the Irish Actors' Equity Association, a regular trade union, belonging to the national trades-union council, and with fraternal ties to its British counterpart. It was therefore possible to apply to this union for help. The grounds for complaint were simple and well within the normal scope of trade union activity. Work had been contracted for (the modifications of the script during rehearsal) and its completion was hindered by the employers' failure to provide satisfactory conditions. In essence this grievance was no different from that of, say, a glass-blower who was asked to work so near the furnace that he was in danger of being overcome by the heat. The glass-blowers' union would have, and indeed often has, taken up such an issue and induced the management to change its working conditions. The authors notified their union of the situation, and declared their plan to go on strike until their demands were met – i.e. until a general company meeting in the theatre was called to discuss (*a*) the meaning, and (*b*) the ensuing interpretation, of the play. At the same time they formally notified both the director of the play, who was also an official of the RSC management, and the representative of British Actors' Equity in the Aldwych company.

The response to this announcement was a wire from the Society of Irish Playwrights (whose headquarters is in Dublin) to the Aldwych, asking for immediate steps to be taken to end the dispute. The Aldwych replied to the SIP with a short message to the effect that they (the SIP) had been misinformed about the situation. The director

of the play then wrote to the authors regretting their decision
to withdraw from the production. He made no reference to their
trade union, or to their announcement that they were on strike,
and appeared to regard their action as merely one of *resignation*,
which his letter implicitly accepted. It still seemed as though he was
expecting them to continue with the cutting of the script. The
authors approached the Equity representative, who called a meeting which was attended by the authors and a large part of the cast.
At this meeting the actors who were there decided to go to the
director and ask if he could not let the general company meeting
take place, as the authors demanded. The director again refused.
The actors were in a weak position here; the only ones with the
power to call such a meeting were the director and his superior, the
artistic director of the RSC. The actors' contracts were up for re-
newal in a few months' time, unemployment in the theatrical profession was at a level close to 90 per cent, and it is understandable
that members of a celebrated subsidised company would think twice
before jeopardising their continued employment over an issue which
neither their current 'classical' environment nor their traditional
British theatrical training equipped them to understand. The authors
did hope, however, that the link between the SIP and Equity would
help the cast pressure the director. They decided to picket at the
stage door of the theatre for as long as work continued – i.e. every
day, about 11–13 hours, until the curtain went up on the opening
performance. (The authors' contracted term of work would have
ended when the curtain rose.)

The picket was joined by a large number of sympathetic fellow-
writers, and other concerned people (letters of support were received
from many more). This resulted in further approaches being made
by the actors to the director, all of them turned down. Some of the
actors began to enter the theatre through the front of the house, to
avoid the embarrassment of passing the picket, while others continually stopped and discussed the dispute with the authors. The
composer and designers, who throughout the dispute associated
themselves strongly with the director in his refusal to throw their
combined work open to analysis and discussion, also evaded the

picket as much as possible. The director never came near the picket and seems actually to have lived inside the theatre throughout this period. His superior (the artistic director) and the literary editor of the RSC paid one visit each to the picket to consider the question of the general company meeting. All they would offer was a private meeting in the administrative office with the artistic director and the director of the play. As it did not appear that anything could be discussed at such a meeting that was not already being discussed on the pavement, the authors rejected the offer as meaningless.

At this point, the shop-steward of the theatre technicians became very concerned about the picket; as a member of what may be called the 'skilled work-force' rather than the 'artistic element', he was well-informed about trade union practice and procedure. He asked the authors to contact the secretary of his own union, as he did not wish the technicians to be suspected of scabbing. The technicians' union immediately took proper action and an official came to the theatre.

This was an important development, for it showed that the technicians' union recognised the right of the playwrights to take industrial action and to call upon other organised workers for support, provided the dispute was officially backed by the SIP. Now the only immediate contact with the SIP was the office of British Equity, whose General Secretary also came to the theatre. A discussion was held between the representatives of Equity and the technicians' union on the one hand, and the theatre management on the other. The General Secretary of Equity then announced that the SIP had told him to instruct the authors to call off their picket; that the authors' action was not officially backed; that they had therefore no right to continue with it; that the Equity members had no right to take any action to support them – their sole right was to rehearse and act the play; and that the only person who had any rights in the matter was the director, who had the right, *as a human being*, to refuse to call a general company meeting if he found it convenient to do so. This failure of Equity to recognise the status of the authors' dispute at once absolved the technicians' union from any further action. The SIP in fact had *not* withdrawn recognition from the authors; and indeed the British Equity officials had *not* been in contact with any representatives of the Society of Irish Playwrights but only with someone in the office of Irish Actors' Equity, who was not authorised to speak for the SIP in this way. But this information did not reach the authors until some time later.

The explanation for such apparent chicanery among union officials lies in the unequal relationship which generally exists between Irish and British labour-organisations. Although Ireland is nominally an independent sovereign state, economically it is still very much a colony of Great Britain. If there is great unemployment among British actors, the situation is far worse in Ireland. It is therefore necessary for Irish actors to emigrate to Britain, but any transference of British actors in the opposite direction would be exceedingly bad for the Irish theatre. Irish Actors' Equity is thus dependent upon British Actors' Equity for the privilege of keeping this resource of emigration available to their members. If Irish Equity refused to co-operate with British Equity over such a matter as the *Island of the Mighty* dispute, it would be perfectly possible for British Equity to move to prevent further incursions of Irish artists into Britain. This coercive situation, however, does not apply to Irish playwrights. Thus British Equity avoided direct contact with the SIP, and relied upon the complicity of Irish Actors' Equity. British Equity, at the same time, because of the high unemployment rate, was not anxious to oppose a powerful subsidised management like the RSC, which provides good long-term contracts for its favoured employees. Also there was a movement afoot within the ranks of British Equity to replace the existing emollient leadership with more militant activists, and any attempt to 'stir up' actors to take any sort of action was strongly deprecated at Equity headquarters. (There was never any question, by the way, of the authors' requesting a sympathetic strike by the Aldwych actors; this had recently been made impossible by the Heath government's Industrial Relations legislation. But there are many forms of effective union pressure short of an outright strike.)

The same day that the unsatisfactory meeting between the management and the union officials took place there arose a new element in the dispute: the authors discovered that while they were on strike the director had cut the play, and the actors were rehearsing the abridged version. This went against all traditional procedure in trade disputes: the actors, by accepting without protest the cuts in the script, were now unwittingly operating as scab labour. So the authors decided to continue their picket, whether or not they were backed by their union. They did not, however, need to prolong their pavement-watch until the opening night. Previews were performed to paying audiences for several evenings before the play was officially opened; the previews were strictly dress rehearsals. One evening a preview was interrupted by some people in the audience who were sympathetic to the authors. They stopped the play and demanded that the authors be brought into the house. From the stage, the director tried to deflect their demand by suggesting it would be better to let the dress rehearsal proceed, and to hold a discussion with the authors after the final curtain. A member of the audience, alarmed at the mood of some of the people in the theatre – and fearing that the police were about to be sent for – went outside to ask the authors to go in and calm down the growing anger. When the authors appeared on the stage they were greeted by a mixed chorus of cheers and rebukes. They realised, however, that the necessary constituents of their general company meeting were all present: the actors and director on the stage, the composer and designers in the auditorium. John Arden asked the audience if they wanted him to speak. He was told 'No' by what appeared to him to be the majority voice of the house; voices in his favour, from the balcony, were drowned out in the uproar. So the authors – deciding that, in effect, they had had their general meeting, and that their part in it had been voted redundant – left the theatre and prepared to go home to Ireland.

On their return to Dublin, they contacted the Chairman of the Society of Irish Playwrights, and obtained assurance of the Society's general and continued support for their cause. He wrote a strong letter, on their behalf, to the London *Times*, defending the right of playwrights to conditions of work which enables them to secure the best possible presentation of their play's meaning. The Chairman also undertook to sort out the dubious circumstances surrounding the communications between British and Irish Actors' Equity officials.

There had been a large number of other letters to the press during the dispute. The RSC had put out a series of justifications and explanations of their part in the argument but they never recognised the right of playwrights to take the trade union action; they never discussed the dispute in terms of a trade dispute but preferred instead to treat it as a matter purely of 'artistic' controversy involving temperamental incompatibilities and other personal issues. They also used a 'Divide-and-Rule' technique, implying that whereas John Arden was a sincere though sadly misled writer of talent, his partner Margaretta D'Arcy was no more than a 'political activist'. She had, they hinted, come over for rehearsals only to sabotage the dignity of the RSC. Of course they were in a dilemma; it was necessary to attack the authors, for the authors were attacking them. But if they accused Arden of being a low-class troublemaker they would make people wonder why they chose to present the play in the first place. But the fact that there were two authors made it possible for the RSC handouts to attack one at the expense of the other, and they naturally chose the more vulnerable of the pair. D'Arcy was: (*a*) female, and (*b*) Irish.

The events at the Aldwych, coincided with unfortunate, serious troubles in Ireland. Bombs had been planted in Dublin, killing and maiming people. The Provisional IRA was at first accused of this but when it became obvious that the advantage of the bombing fell to the ruling party in the Dublin government and the British government in Westminster, it was generally accepted that someone else had planted the explosives. The bombs effectively caused the opposition in the Dublin Parliament to withdraw their promise to vote against a noxious bill called the 'Offences Against the State (Amendment) Act'. By their withdrawal the bill was passed and the life of the government prolonged (for it was understood that had the bill failed in Parliament the Prime Minister would have called a General Election). The effect of this bill was to equip the government with police-state powers not unlike those in British-controlled Northern Ireland or even Rhodesia, South Africa, Greece and Brazil. There are now many prisoners held in Irish jails on no stronger evidence than the word of a police officer that he believes they belong to subversive organisations. No jury is necessary in these trials, and it is a dangerous situation as well as a national disgrace. While all this was going on in Ireland, a paragraph appeared in the London *Times* associating Margaretta D'Arcy with the (Official) Sinn Fein – a party only too easily confused by British Readers with the Provisional IRA. These political side-swipes did not much affect the course of the Aldwych dispute. But coincidentally something else happened with grave effects to the authors' careers.

A play by Arden and D'Arcy – *The Ballygombeen Bequest* – had been running for some months in the provinces. It now returned to London for a short season in a fringe-theatre. The day after the paragraph appeared in *The Times*, which was also the day of the Aldwych opening, the 7/84 Company (producers of *Ballygombeen*) received a communication from a firm of lawyers, informing them that an action for slander against Arden/D'Arcy was to be taken in connection with this play: and that if *Ballygombeen* were not at once taken from the boards, 7/84 would find themselves a party to the suit. They felt they had no option but to comply, and the performances of the play ended that day. The actors did not lose financially by this, as they were paid up to the date when they would anyway have concluded their engagement: but it will be readily understood that such a situation was not good for the company, and it did not help the authors to establish the serious principles of their case against the Aldwych. 'If such persons are allowed to bring their ideas anywhere near a stage,' many people must have thought, 'they will inevitably create disruption and unprofessional scandal'. 7/84, in contrast to the RSC, were a politically-orientated company; and the theme of *Ballygombeen* was the current troubles in Ireland . . .

At the same time the RSC declared that they would allow a discussion after the final curtain on The Island's opening night.

Presumably they hoped people would read into this announcement that they were a thoroughly liberal organisation, keen on having all sides of the question ventilated. But they damaged this impression by: (*a*) not inviting the authors to the discussion (an announcement in the *Times*' correspondence columns was their only way of knowing about the meeting), and (*b*) referring in their statement to only one author, John Arden, thus carrying on the discriminatory tone of their previous propaganda. The authors disregarded this announcement, not only because of its irregular form, but also because they considered the dress rehearsal interruption a clear indication of the Aldwych stage's value as a forum for their grievances – particularly in view of the RSC administration's refusal to make any serious effort to settle their strike.

The intransigence of the RSC was but one symptom of a growing tendency, in the British subsidised theatre, to fall back, in any difficulty, upon a bureaucratic and hierarchical set of formulae. The directors in such institutions are themselves becoming more bureaucrat than artist; and in *The Island* case the confusion of roles, in the single personality shared by the director of the play and the official of the theatre, was the principal reason why the authors were forced to use the tactics of a trade dispute. The director in question clearly preferred to be seen as a misunderstood artist; but he behaved like a disaffected employer, 'pulling rank' on his actors instead of respecting that delicate trust which should inform the relations between a cast and their artistic co-ordinator. This attitude in the theatre came into prominence at about the same time as the Tory government under Edward Heath set itself a policy of overall inflexibility in the face of labour unrest and Irish 'rebellion'. The result, in public life, was a hardening of resistance by the trade unions and the Six-County Republicans. In the theatre we have since seen a similar increase of militancy which has split Equity upon overt political lines, and which has gravely disturbed whatever complacency may have remained among managements. If authors as well as actors were to become part of the general disaffection, then the directors must be ready to protect themselves

against their 'arbitrary demands'. If a director were to link himself
into a regular, if unofficial, partnership with a designer, it would be
easier for the pair of them to agree on the mode of presentation of
any particular play without too much reference to the playwright's
intentions: and in the case of *The Island* something like this
appears to have happened. The team here extended itself to include
the composer – he was shortly afterwards working on an entertainment at Covent Garden to celebrate the entry of Great Britain into
the Common Market: which would indicate no inconsistency in
his attitude towards authoritative combination. (The Common
Market, of course, as presently constituted, is the apotheosis of the
kind of bureaucratic intransigence we have been describing, and is
set up so as to minimise, on an international scale, the influence
and power of organised labour.)

It is only recently that playwrights in Ireland have been able to
operate – in a very limited form – as members of 'organised labour'.
There is no British equivalent to the SIP. Before Arden and D'Arcy
returned to Ireland after the Aldwych dispute they took part in a
meeting of British dramatists, called as the first step in the formation
of a Playwrights' Trade Union. At the time of writing it is not
possible to predict the success of this attempt.* But the SIP already
has had a number of unquestionable successes in their dealings with
the Dublin managements, where of course they are on their home
ground and can muster forces in a way not possible when the dispute is in England.

The role of the playwright in the theatre should no longer be left
to the mercy of the good feeling of individual directors and administrators. The fact, of course, that Arden and D'Arcy were
paid for their work at the rehearsals of *The Island* was at first sight
a most encouraging step forward; but the standard contract under
which this arrangement was negotiated was hopelessly out-of-date
in its assumptions, and the whole area of 'what happens if they fail
to agree?' was left unprovided for. In the contemporary state of
monopoly-capitalist-bureaucratic affairs, where a sort of ferocious
yet defensive voracity prevails, the so-called 'gentleman's agreement'

* see page 158

can no longer be trusted. The RSC regarded as *gentlemanly* their refusal to allow the playwrights practical contact with all the creative forces at work on the play, but a strike-picket was seen as *ungentlemanly*, to be dismissed with opprobrium and smeared with every disagreeable half-truth that could be summoned from theatrical gossip and political scandal about the authors' activities. The solution devised in the United States is to put the author under contract as a co-director of his new play; this places control of the play's meaning where it belongs, and leaves the *interpretation* of the play to the director. It may be argued – and indeed was, at the meeting of British playwrights mentioned above – that these tabulated distinctions cannot possibly be made in an art form so ephemeral and dependent upon individual inspiration as the theatre. But where the directors, designers and composers all regard themselves as part of the management of the company and have thus combined their creative influences with far more potent financial influence of the theatre's front office, the playwrights are left sadly unprotected and must seize the weapons of defence available to them. A union linked to the national trade union movement would be an obvious strength – at least in the British context.* (Things may be somewhat different in the United States, where labour organising has taken on a chauvinistic right-wing tinge ever since the purging of so-called subversive elements from the unions shortly after World War II. But it may well be that the Nixon administration, similar in many ways to the Heath cabal, will bring about a change of direction here.)

Shortly after the Aldwych affair, Arden and D'Arcy went to work for a few months at the University of California, Davis. The difficulties they met with there are described in another essay in this book: but it was perhaps significant that press reports of the controversy with the RSC had reached America before they did, and materially contributed to the atmosphere of political distrust with

*The British Society of Authors was unable to help in the Aldwych dispute. It is inhibited by the terms of its foundation from operating as a trade union.

which their project (on James Connolly and the American Labour Movement) was greeted.

But what about the actual production of *The Island of the Mighty* at the Aldwych? Did it, in any way, after all the trouble, recapture any of the authors' intentions? They do not know: they never saw it. They had their names removed from the programmes, in the hope that the critics and the public would realise what was on the stage was alone the work of the RSC – based admittedly upon an Arden/D'Arcy script – but abridged and interpreted finally without reference to the writers and their desired meaning. Whatever individuals in the audience may have thought, the critics refused to recognise this, and went on to review the play as if the authors had never spent the last two weeks of rehearsal pacing a wet pavement outside the stage door. The one exception to this was the critic of the (Communist) *Morning Star*, who telephoned the authors and asked them their views about the opening. When they said they had repudiated the production he said he would not review it and did not. In general the reviews were bad, which was no surprise considering the way the play looked at the first run-through and the director's obvious intention to carry it out along the same lines. Attendance, too, was very poor.

Whatever the original hopes of the director and those who supported him in his intransigence, they were certainly not achieved. The play was successful neither artistically nor commercially, and both sides of the dispute lost money over the business. A theatre run with such insensitivity towards good labour-relations and with such arrogant obstinacy on the part of its administration may well find itself regarded as an example of bad and inefficient management in other aspects of its affairs. Under the prevailing economic conditions, we are continually told, bad management must be eliminated. Mergers and takeovers, closures and lay-offs, are being threatened on all sides. Indeed, at the time of writing, a merger between the RSC and the other big subsidised British theatre, the National, has been hinted at more than once. Such a 'rationalism' would no doubt carry with it the eventual loss of jobs – it always does. But who, except those thrown out of work, will really give a damn? A national theatre has one main purpose: artistic prestige. If that purpose is attained the subsidies will continue despite financial loss, provided the loss is not too outrageous. After *The Island of the Mighty* the prestige of the Aldwych has at least suffered some dilution. There may, of course, even in 1972, have been those expecting something more than mere prestige, a sense, perhaps, of creative adventure and a belief in the content of the plays selected for performance. Nothing done by the Aldwych management in this affair confirmed such expectations.

# Playwrights and Play-Writers

1. A theatrical *happening* ... is a long seance, whose contours should be shaped by the cast, together with the author. The artist organises the separate world of the stage, expressing it by means of his own signs; the actor – by his actions, not necessarily imitating life verbatim. Together they create a world not limited to any historically determined place and time, but rather expressed in a conceptual way. The word lives within the structure of this theatre as one of its permanent, meaningful and equal elements ... Today we must write of productions, not plays.

   *Józef Szajna*

2. The emphasis on movement has led Szajna to reinterpret and redefine the classics, especially *Faust* and *The Divine Comedy* ... It is at moments like this that Szajna becomes more than a prophet or a messiah. Art traverses the boundaries of being and not being, of affirmation and rejection. Theatre becomes conflict: the rest is left to man's conscience.

   *E. J. Czerwiński*

3. All the important work on *A Midsummer Night's Dream* was based on my convincing the actors that there were two plays; one was what we call the secret play ... The other play ... has been discussed and worked over intellectually. *That* play is like

dough that's been worked over and kneaded, but the yeast was the sort of sensitivity that enables the actors to pick up the secret play – which runs parallel and through the apparent play – and to share their perception with the audience.

*Peter Brook*

4. On the face of it, scripts have clearly not been a compelling pre-occupation of current experimental theatre ... Their fate has been the aspect least provided for, seeming at times a corruption of the whole point of avant-garde theatre, which believes itself to be striving for a kind of reclamation of gesture from action ... I attended one of the Grotowski productions with Jan Kott, whose primary language is, of course, Polish. I regretted being cut off from the language being spoken by the performers, and at one point I asked Kott what more was happening in the action department than was explicated in the printed programme. 'How should I know? I can't understand the words,' he replied ...

*Donald M. Kaplan*

5. Just as new music has reacted against the tyranny of the printed score, new theatre has rejected the supremacy of text in favour of a complex information structure that includes movement, gesture and non-verbal sound.

*Paul Epstein*

6. I feel personally that I've got back to when I was ten years old and could react simply and directly before I was fucked up by twenty years' schooling and conditioning – you know the way young kids' paintings are so much better than older kids'. We don't work out our images rationally; we just get them to a point where they are right. I'm very political and I suppose most of the others are 'Left' in a sort of non-verbalised way. They know instinctively that people are repressed in our society and are against it. It represents quite a threat to the existing order of things for twenty or thirty people playing musical instruments

and wearing fantastic costumes to suddenly appear and march through the streets in an apparently anarchic fashion.

*John Fox*

The above quotations, selected at random and admittedly out-of-context, are opinions upon modern theatre expressed by (1) a Polish Director, (2) a Polish Critic, (3) a British Director, (4) an American Psychoanalyst, (5) an American Composer and (6) a British Theatre/Event Group Co-ordinator. They all seem to agree on one thing: that the theatre today has little or no use for the old idea of a play-text consisting of a series of speeches interspersed by a few 'stage-directions'. Indeed so strong has become the reaction to this 'old idea' that the tone of polemic can grow heated, if not abusive. Words and phrases like 'non-verbalised', 'tyranny', 'corruption', 'fucked up by twenty years' schooling' are frequent; and such affirmations as 'more than a prophet, or a messiah', 'the sort of sensitivity that enables the actors . . .' (implying perhaps that most actors are not normally required to develop much sensitivity while working on conventional scripts in a conventional manner) testify to an almost ideological intensity of debate. If the sight of a regular scripted play arouses emotions of rejection and even disgust, are we to assume that recent generations of theatre-workers have hit on something that remained hidden throughout the ages which produced a Shaw, an Ibsen, a Shakespeare? That the body of European classical theatre was in fact deficient in a major dimension of dramaturgy – that playwrights traditionally concerned themselves only with verbal statement and neglected all those other aspects of their art – such as movement, abstract sound, sculptural or painterly values of spectacle? Leaving these essentials of the three-dimensional theatre to the ad hoc improvisations of actors, scene-painters, musical-directors – and so on?

If this is so, if the Playwright is indeed merely one, and a rather inferior, outmoded, one, among the total creative crew that presents the finished art-work, then clearly the time has come to redistribute the honours. A larger and a better artist must from now on be held responsible as prime mover towards whatever importance the theatre may still have for us. Now the larger and better artist can be either an individual, or a collective. If a collective, then it will not matter how much or how little attention is paid to *scripting* the play, provided the final result works, because the writer will be merely the servant of the entire group, and will write down whatever has been mutually determined upon in the course of the general work. But there are many alleged collectives which in fact are delusory. Their work has the appearance of communal effort: but has really been conceived, controlled and brought to fruition by one concealed individual – who may have been functioning as a writer, a designer, a co-ordinator, an actor or – a Director. And where there is not even the pretence of collective work, it is more and more probable these days that the moving spirit behind the artistic creation is that of a Director. Certainly, whatever the back-stage reality, it is the Director who receives the greater part of the acclaim in the work of the 'high-art' theatre of the present time. One hears far more frequently that such-and-such a theatre is presenting 'A's production of Play B by Author C, with Actor D in the leading role', rather than 'Play B by Author C, acted by D and directed by A' or 'D in the lead in Play B, by C, directed by A . . .' When Arts Councils and Cultural Ministries give grants to companies to travel abroad for international festivals, they like to have a proven name to guarantee their financial returns and critical prestige: and the name is more often that of a Director – sometimes an Actor – very very rarely a Playwright.

This is convenient, because international theatre is normally regarded as a peaceful and non-controversial area of world intercourse. Directors, on the whole, may be trusted to keep it so. There is more likelihood that hackles will be raised by the content of plays than by their interpretations. The Director of an awkward script can be expected to modify it where its Author might cavil. Plays written in words *say* things; there is always the danger that some of those things would be better left unsaid. Plays composed in 'non-verbalised' images *hint* at things: and a saving ambiguity can thus be pleaded if offence should be taken. If there is no Playwright, but merely a Director and Actors developing 'non verbalised' images in

an 'integrated' manner 'not limited by place and time', the style of
the presentation is likely to be so abstracted and so dependent upon
generalised emotional responses rather than precise analysis that
very few people (in any form of society sufficiently liberal to permit
theatres at all) could possibly be upset. Also, as the Director *directs*
Actors upon the stage, it is no great step to have the same person
*direct* them administratively as well; and so two birds are killed
with a single stone – the artistic *and bureaucratic* control of the
company are securely placed in the same pair of hands. The owner
of the hands can thus choose or not choose to present the work of
any Author or none, according to taste – and political judgement.

So in the end the international theatre-group, swooping by
jumbo-jet from one cultural function to another all over the world,
has ceased to attempt to communicate specific ideas about anything
to anybody – a non-verbal compost of currently-received physical
images which can mean all things to all men is trundled from stage
to stage between Tokyo and Nancy, Zagreb and Singapore. 'Controversy', if aroused at all, is set afoot only by such classless generali-
ties as naked bodies, cursorily-motivated violence, and a broad
demonstration of 'compassion for the human condition'. Compassion for the victims of one particular political system, violence
directed against one particular group of exploiters (or on behalf of
one particular group of exploiters), nudity in defiance of the re-
pressive rules of one particular religion, are concepts not welcome
in this atmosphere of mutual evasion: in any case to be particular
would be 'limiting' to the artists . . .

This emasculating elevation of the Director above the Playwright and above the Actor is a comparatively modern phenomenon.
Until the second half of the nineteenth century there was virtually
no such official as the Director in the business at all. The function
was first embodied in the person of the Duke of Saxe-Meiningen,
who determined to rid his court theatre of the debasing influence
of the overblown leading-actor. Subordinate characters and crowds
were being shuffled on and off the scene without any care for their
contribution to the play as a whole, while the Mr and Mrs Crummles
of the day, better-dressed and more fully rehearsed than anyone else,

obtrusively ate up the applause from the centre of the stage. The Duke was particularly fond of Shakespeare; and he set about a series of Shakespearian productions in which an equal amount of attention was applied to the artistry of every member of the cast. Crowds for the first time in recent theatre history were controlled as an integral part of every scene they belonged to – not by a fellow-actor standing on the same stage (as had been the case with the conscientious productions of Charles Kean, for example) but by an overall co-ordinator seated in the auditorium, who could relate the groupings and movements absolutely from the outside. Being a Duke, this new 'Director' really could *direct*: Crummles and his like were his social inferiors as well as his artistic employees, and the modern 'integrated ensemble' was launched into a sea of well-conditioned German deference. It was at once seen how beneficial for Shakespearian revival was this new method of work. It was suddenly apparent that the plays had been written for a *company* and not for a pair of stars.

And yet, there is no record of any Director having been employed at The Globe. As far as we know, a company of Actors, with one or two principals (whose names – Burbage, Lowin, Kemp, et al. – became household words in their own time), was capable of mounting these plays by its own unaided efforts, with the 'menial' assistance of the Prompter or the Stage-manager – and no doubt some advice from the Poet. That the manner of production was satisfactory to Shakespeare and to most of his fellow-writers may be deduced from the fact that throughout their careers they continued to write large-scale complex works, of increasing sophistication, which no experienced Playwright would ever dream of offering – at any rate, more than once – to a self-assertive manager of the later Crummles type. Józef Szajna's requirements were in fact met by the Elizabethan-Jacobeans; and yet it is obvious from the briefest knowledge of the plays that there was never any question of 'scripts not being a compelling preoccupation' in that theatre. Verbally the work has never been excelled. And it is today the very verbal intensity of the Shakespearian school of playwriting that is so dismissively regarded by avant-garde practitioners. A wheel of some sort appears to have come full circle. It would perhaps be advantageous to examine Shakespeare's dramaturgy a little more closely and to find out (from the texts themselves, and from what is known – or may fairly be assumed – about actual production customs) just how the Poets related themselves and their words to the three-dimensional values of the play-in-performance. If this can be done, even to a small extent, it might be possible to rid ourselves of a good deal of the humbug that surrounds the modern 'art-theatre' and its social make-up, with the eventual aim of re-establishing the Playwright in a useful and fulfilling role.

Given the large repertoire of an Elizabethan theatre, and the practice of presenting a different play each afternoon instead of continuous runs, it looks as though the normal period of rehearsal for a new piece could not have been much longer than two weeks. 'Fortnightly rep' nowadays is regarded as an undesirable arrangement, only indulged in when the resources of the company are very limited. Three weeks for a full-length play is normal, or four in a well-subsidised establishment. Two weeks' rehearsal makes for unimaginative trick-filled acting, tatty décor, stereotyped interpretation of theme. A company restricted to it in continuous repertory will not select 'difficult' plays – well-known and proven successes are more likely to work under these summary conditions. If new plays are put on they will either be chosen for their simplicity of content or they will be presented so abruptly that half of the Author's intentions will be missed. It is hard to believe that Shakespeare's mature writing was intended for such circumstances. A modern Director presenting *King Lear* is going to take longer than two weeks to determine his lines of work before he even selects his actors. And when plays of this profundity were new to everyone save the Author, the difficulty would have been enormously multiplied. There is also the added obstacle of the afternoon performance. In a modern rep, the theatre is available for rehearsal all day except maybe twice a week when there are matinees; at The Globe, only the mornings would have been free. After the show the dark open theatre would have had to be illuminated; the cost of lighting – and probably heating – would have been a deterrent, and even not-very-respectable people like actors would have avoided the Bankside after sunset. Public houses could have been used, but surely only for rehearsing the spoken lines – entire productions would not have been set up in the snug? But supposing the *rehearsal of the spoken lines* was the main need of the company? If so, then some small rented space in a public house or anywhere else would have been entirely adequate.

I believe that this is what must in fact have happened. The principle task confronting the Elizabethan Actor was to make himself word-perfect, and then to establish the correct verbal interpretation of his role with his colleagues, and – in the case of a new play – with the *Author* at hand to explain the required shades of meaning. The old style of reproducing scripts, each Actor being given only the lines of his own part with attached cues, would appear to confirm this. We are told, for instance, that Ben Jonson, as an actor, was not talented, but that he was effective at instructing the cast of his plays. It cannot be that he was expected to *direct* (in the modern sense) a full production of *Volpone* in two weeks. But if he did not do this, who did? The leading Actor – Burbage, or whoever – would certainly have had some say in it, but as the plays generally were ensemble works, it would have involved much more than an early-nineteenth-century disposal of the small-part men as feeds around the elbows of the star. There was of course a Stage-manager, and a Stage-carpenter: but until Inigo Jones began to develop his elaborate art-work at the court-masques and thereby raised the social status of these crafts, the persons employed remained anonymous and clearly subordinate in the overall theatre hierarchy. The answer must be that all the company, as a company, created the production together in conditions of reasonable artistic harmony.

Each member – Actor, Hired-man, juvenile Apprentice, Stage-manager, Stage-carpenter or Musician – must have known without having to be told exactly what to do in any given situation that was likely to arise. An Actor, for example, would have understood that if he were cast as one of the Ambassadors in *Hamlet* (Act I Scene 2, Act II Scene 2) he would have to enter at a particular door, take up

a particular position on the stage, address his remarks to the King
in a particular way, and go out again at a particular door – that all
this business was the regular way in which Ambassadors in plays
carried on, and that if for any reason there were to be any variations the Author would make them clear at the first reading of the
script. (If the Author, like Shakespeare, was a reliable professional,
variations would be rare. One suspects that such Playwrights as
Greene, with only one foot in the theatre and the other one in
journalism or pick-pocketing or worse, might have difficulties
here; and this may be one reason why Greene in the end became
disillusioned with the players. His stage-directions tend to be
augmented by phrases like 'if you can conveniently', suggesting a
dilettante approach.) The role of an Ambassador, moreover, would
carry with it no problems about what to wear, or what sort of make-
up to put on. In the tiring-house there would be a set of stock
costumes labelled 'Ambassadors etc.' or something similar : and all
the Actor need do would be to select one that fitted him. If it did not
fit, there would be an adjustment to be made by the wardrobe
keeper, but there would certainly be no question of *designing* a
special dress. The Author would have already have explained
whether the play was to be got up in ordinary clothes (*Hamlet*),
Roman clothes (*Julius Caesar*), or Turkish clothes (*Tamburlaine*).
These stylised outfits would no doubt be stored in batches, and
would include nearly everything that would be needed for any
play in each mode. There were also, of course, special-effect costumes, such as Caliban's fish-suit, and Rumour's garment painted
full of tongues, which might have to be purpose-made, but which,
once acquired, would do for any play where something of the sort
was wanted. Make-up must have been very conventionalised, as
many Actors played several roles in the one play, and they could
not be expected to involve themselves in elaborate facial disguises,
if the changes were at all rapid.

All this would be made much easier by the constant repetition in
Elizabethan plays of a whole range of stock-scenes. I do not mean that
the *content* of the scenes is stock – Shakespeare's work of course is
filled with unpredictable dramatic surprises – but the overall concept

is one of rule-of-thumb notation. A king on his throne receives
Ambassadors, addresses Counsellors, adjudicates dynastic problems.
The *Hamlet* scenes mentioned above fall into this category. So does
the first scene of *Richard II* (Bolingbroke's challenge to Mowbray,
with the King looking on); so does Act II Scene 1 of *Julius Caesar*
(the assassination). The actions covered in each of these scenes are
radically different: the presentation would have been identical. The
Stage-manager would place the throne where it was always placed
for such episodes; and the Actors would place themselves in such
relation to the throne as the respective importance of their roles demanded. Would Hamlet in his first scene have an unprecedented
position? He has asides to deliver, and, being the protagonist, he will
be expected to dominate the stage from his first entrance. Something special might have had to be worked out here. But as he was
the only character with any sort of blocking-problem, not much
time need have been wasted. Who would have determined the
'relative importance of the roles' for the rest of the cast? The Actors'
own hierarchical status in the company would have no doubt over-
ridden any ambiguity in the text. Polonius obviously would have
taken a better position than Voltimand: but between Voltimand
and Cornelius seniority in the profession could have had the last
word. Any quarrels, and the Stage-manager would be called in to
arbitrate. Any arguments about sight-lines or masking, and again
the Stage-manager would make the necessary adjustments. The
whole thing could be fixed up from the start in perhaps ten minutes
with no preparatory planning at all. Similar stock-scenes were the
Battle between Two Armies, with military entrances, drum and
colours; the Grassy Bank reclining scene (Titania and Bottom, the
Murder of Gonzago, very possibly the death of Cassius); the Bed-
room Scene (Imogen, Desdemona, Volpone), the Court-entertain-
ment scene (the play in *Hamlet*, the fencing-match in *Hamlet*, the
fight at barriers in *The White Devil*, the masque in *Henry VIII* –
as well as innumerable last acts throughout all Jacobean tragedy).

   The important phrase to bear in mind is 'rule-of-thumb'. Acting
was a traditional craft, like carpentry, or goldsmith-work, and the
Apprentices were taught from the beginning of their careers the

standard craftsman's response to standard situations. In the building trade throughout the Middle Ages down to the arrival of the
Italianate Architect in the sixteenth century, such structural systems as vaulting, buttressing, or the layout of frame-timbers re-
cognisably followed the same unwritten principles from Cracow
to Barcelona. Of course details of ornament varied from place to
place, and the overall plan of a building would be affected by
regional requirements: but in general a qualified mason from any
country in Christendom would have been able without much difficulty to fulfil contracts alongside local labour on any site he chose
to visit in any land. Similarly an English Actor in the period concluded by the Civil War could accept work in any company in any
town in any Playwright's play and not have to change his working
routine, or accommodate himself to the personality of a 'New
Director'. By the same token, any Playwright told the size of the
company and the type of story they wanted dramatising would have
at his disposal a complete series of received conventions into which
he could fit his narrative – a process carried out by his professional
sub-conscious – because there were virtually no alternative artistic
modes from which he could choose. He *could* choose verse or prose,
rhymed verse or blank verse, simple statement or elaborate imagery;
and obviously he could write badly or well within this framework –
but as far as stage-craft went, the Actors had developed their system
without much formal theorising; hand to mouth, as it were, over a
period of three or four generations before the heyday of Shakespeare. Increasing financial success had proved the value of their
methods, and there was therefore no incentive for radical innovation.

A pointer to this craft-guild-orientated tradition is the way in
which the lists of *dramatis personae* were laid out in published play-
texts for many years, even down to the twentieth century. Instead
of a list 'in order of appearance', or even in order of importance of
all the characters, the *male* roles were placed in one block, followed
by the *female*. Each sex-group was printed according to social rank,
starting with a King or a Queen and ending with supernumeraries
– peasants, soldiers, etc., or nymphs, concubines, virgins ... This
was not a male-chauvinist display so much as a natural reflection

of the structure of the company before the introduction of actresses. The female roles were played by boys, who were Apprentices, and therefore not entitled to full billing.

It may be thought that such a rigid hierarchy of working relationships would make for artistic conservatism, but again the evidence of the plays proves that this could not have been the case. If Burbage, for example, had been content with the comparatively crude effects of Richard III, it is unlikely that the subtleties of Macbeth would have been offered him. But then it must be remembered that Burbage was not an *Actor-manager* concerned with the public presentation of his own ego. He was one among several Shareholders who controlled the artistic and financial destinies of the company – and another Shareholder was Shakespeare himself. There was a mutual dependence of the Actors upon the Poet, and vice versa, for the common advantage of the entire group. It is true that most Playwrights were not members of acting-companies in this way; but many of them seem to have been regularly connected with one company or another, undertaking to supply scripts for an agreed fee at regular intervals. Such an arrangement must have brought the Dramatist continually and closely in touch with the work of rehearsal. There was no question of his living and writing quite isolated from the active theatre, only attending rehearsals as a kind of embarrassed client of the Director, unable to address the Actors except by courtesy of the Director, and finding the 'original creative ideas' of Director, Designer, Musical Director, Choreographer, etc., etc. all coming up between him and his potential audience like the train of ghosts on Bosworth Field. There were no 'original creative ideas' except the play itself – but there was a group of well-practised professionals who had at their fingertips every technique needed to make the play work.

In any new play the only new element the Actors would require to master from scratch would be the words themselves; and two weeks or so would have been sufficient for this. Character-interpretation was a function of the rhythm of the words. Once the Author and the Actor together had established what this rhythm was meant to be, the traditional blocking and stage-business would combine

with the rhetoric to present a personality both socially and psychologically plausible to the public. The better the Actor, the more
subtle his speech-technique, and the more complex the rhythms
available to the Poet who wrote his lines.

There was in fact a kind of *dual structure* to the drama of the
time: the structure privately developed by the Playwright in his
study, which was worked out of words, metre, metaphor and the
other tools of a poet's skill; and the structure communally imposed
by the company at work in the theatre – entrances, exits, solo scenes,
duologues, crowd scenes, and all the resources of the back-stage
workshop with its store of emblematic thrones, dragons, castle walls,
ships, flying cranes, and so on. These two structures were brought
together to create a narrative. However capable the Poet might have
been at handling his words, unless he also knew how to activate the
traditional stagecraft, his plays would not succeed. But once he *did*
know this, he could call upon the devices of the theatre to illumi-
nate his theme as freely and as fruitfully as he called upon the
mythology of Ovid or the dogma of the Bible to invigorate his
dialogue.

Much of the scholarship applied to Elizabethan dramatists has
ignored this dual structure. Either the works have been appreciated
as literary texts, or they have been analysed as evidence for historical
reconstruction of theatre buildings and actors' practice; but the
necessary combination of the two approaches has been rare. I suspect
that this is due to the close relationship that has obtained between
the Shakespearian critic and the current conventions of the theatre.
In the time of the great Actor-managers, from Kemble to Beerbohm
Tree, the emphasis of criticism was upon the Characters of the Plays.
Bradley's essays are essentially a more scholarly development of
Hazlitt's – and if Hazlitt was affected by the performances of Kean,
so Bradley cannot have been ignorant of Sir Henry Irving. The acting was individualistic, the criticism accordingly presented Shakespeare as primarily concerned with individual portrait-drawing. At
the same time, his language was understood as a means of affording
the individual Actor full scope for declamation: on a large gaslit
stage, surrounded by archaeologically justified décor, in a play

continually broken by scene-changes into a series of static set-pieces. William Poel, at the end of the Victorian period, rediscovered what he termed the 'tunes' of the plays – he recognised the verse patterns as a dynamic framework for a continuous narrative, and he believed, rather misleadingly, that this narrative was intended for performance on a bare platform. The richness of Shakespeare's language was thus thought of as a compensation for visual nullity. At the beginning of this century, therefore, two styles of production existed side-by-side – the last lush hangover of the Irving-Tree manner; and the Poelite purism, suitable for the intellectual élite of the Stage Societies, but not appealing to the general public. In time the general public, responsive to propaganda from informed critics such as Bernard Shaw, began to weary of the Actor-managers' *art-pompier*; but they were still repelled by Poel's asceticism.

So a third, compromise, style appeared, developed by Gordon Craig and Granville-Barker, and supplementing the new-found, fluid totality of the texts with an equally new-found type of décor – non-naturalistic, and belonging firmly to the era of post-impressionism. With variations, this *directorial* approach (for it came shortly after the arrival of Saxe-Meiningen's ideas into the British commercial theatre) has continued to the present day. Parallel with it, influencing it and being influenced by it, arose a new critical concentration upon the imagery of the Playwright's language. Caroline Spurgeon's important work on this subject* drew inspiration from the contemporary techniques of the Yeats/Eliot/Pound school of poetry, and she discovered an entire, sub-conscious system of allusive metaphor running right through the play-texts.

For instance, in *Hamlet* there is regular mention of disease and bodily corruption. This does not contribute to the plot – no character is actually shown to be ill (except King Hamlet after his poisoning, and the other poisoned persons in Act V): but 'hectic in my blood', 'growing to a pleurisy', 'to the quick o' the ulcer', 'skin and film the ulcerous place', and many other references, almost casually dropped into the dialogue, all confirm the general impression that

* *Shakespeare's Imagery and What It Tells Us,* Cambridge, 1935.

something 'rotten in the state of Denmark' is as much a physical as a moral decay. Similarly, *Othello* is filled with hints of oriental exotica, and *Macbeth* with images of blood, night, flame and fog. Now when the plays are presented with Directors and Designers combining to provide their own 'creative interpretation' of the themes, this verbal imagery remains a constant – always lodged in the text – but its visual complement differs from one production to another, and becomes merely ephemeral. Shakespeare in Watteau-style, Shakespeare in black-and-white, Shakespeare all in rope or leather, Shakespeare in modern dress, Artaud-style Shakespeare, Brechtian Shakespeare, hippie-Shakespeare – each new bright idea enlivens the stage and perhaps the audience for as long as the box-office keeps open, and then disappears into the illustrated pages of the theatre magazines and the coffee-table souvenir books.

Because the *appearance* of the play is ephemeral, the academic critics must tend to disregard it, and elevate the *verbal meaning* of the play as the main matter of their work. Their work is then studied in schools and colleges, and generations of students are thus induced to dissociate the two interdependent elements of theatre. As a practising Playwright, I have found that this dissociation applies to more than Shakespeare. I frequently receive letters from students who are reading one or other of my plays as part of their course: there are many queries for me to answer about my use of language and my imagery and the characters I have portrayed; but nearly always the plays themselves are treated as one might treat a novel – a story that exists in its own right quite divorced from its practical shape as a piece of theatre craftwork. The writers of these letters no doubt assume that it is not me, the Playwright, who should be questioned about stagecraft, but the Director who presented the plays and determined on my behalf their visual qualities and physical movement. In so far as I have had plays presented in the ordinary professional theatre, with Directors and Designers assigned to them by management, the students' assumptions are justified. But as long as such assumptions *are* justified in the modern theatre, so long will the avant-garde feel the need to call for an end to the tyranny of the literary text. Their instinct is correct.

They see a departmentalised, bureaucratic theatre-system laying its heavy hand on true imaginative flow; and they yearn to break away from it. But they also make the mistake of concluding that the Playwright not only is, but always has been, largely to blame for this. The passivity of such modern Writers as myself in the face of Directorial power is unhistorically attributed to Shakespeare and other classical Dramatists – Molière, Actor and Company Shareholder, is a similar example – and the idea is allowed to evolve that the only way to save the theatre from its moribund state is to downgrade the script and to concentrate entirely upon the 'vital' values of performance.

To understand the values of performance which Shakespeare not only understood, but included among and between the lines of his scripts, we must first recognise that there are two classes of imagery in his published works. There is the verbal imagery, already very well explored by critics; and there is the visual – which follows similar patterns of continuous subconscious allusion, and which can be traced by examination of what actually *happens* in the plays, rather than what is *said* by the characters to happen. Our means of discovering this is to relate the dialogue to the stage-directions. In the First Folio, which, with all its faults, is the authorised text of the company to which Shakespeare belonged, there are not many stage-directions – traditional work-methods of the Actors made it unnecessary for an experienced Author to elaborate on such matters for his colleagues, and the plays were written out for performance rather than for the reader. Sometimes the stage-directions which are missing can be deduced from the subsequent dialogue.

We must always bear in mind the recent researches of Glynne Wickham, Walter Hodges and Richard Southern, who have very fully refuted the Poel idea of a bare stage. The Globe was well equipped with solidly constructed and decorative stock-properties, not for a naturalistic scenic background, but for an emblematic series of notations enhancing the meaning of successive episodes.

A good play to examine is *Hamlet*. C. S. Lewis has written a monograph entitled *Hamlet, Prince or Poem?* Lewis was a follower of the verbal-imagery school of criticism, and concerned to counterbalance the excesses of Bradleian character-analysis. He speaks of a central image of the play being a lobby, in which a young man in black, his stockings coming down, wanders for hours together. This sounds a little like my idea of Shakespeare's inherent *visual* image-pattern: but not quite. The lobby and the hours are *described* in the dialogue, rather than shown directly, and we derive this poignant picture through the response of our imaginations to the spoken word. Upon Hamlet's actual entrance (Act II Scene 2) the most obvious visual effect is not the length of time he has been in the lobby (offstage?) but the book he is specified as reading. The very sight of the book tells us something of his melancholy: but not exactly what Polonius has communicated to the King. This slight difference between visual and verbal image not only fills out the portrait of Hamlet, but brings the action a step further forward – the book is to be used later on in the scene ('What do you read, my lord?') and so has a dynamic function in relation to the play as a whole. If C. S. Lewis had taken account of the stage-direction as well as Polonius's description, he might have found that *Hamlet, Prince, Poem or Play?* would have been a more appropriate title.

There are other visual leitmotiv images throughout the play. One, possibly the most famous Shakespearian image of all, is Hamlet holding the Skull. Or rather, as our eyes do not of themselves tell us the name of the character whom we watch on the stage: 'The Young Man in Black, holding the Skull'. This happens in the graveyard scene (Act V Scene 1), and in many productions a tradition is followed which makes Hamlet toss away the skull when he says 'And smelt so? Puh.' That this is not a modern habit is proved by the mention of it in Dickens's *Great Expectations* (Chapter 31):

'I believe it is well-known in a constitutional country that Mr Wopsle could not possibly have returned the skull, after moralising over it, without dusting his fingers on a white napkin taken from his breast ...'

But, whenever the Actors first began this naturalistic bit of business, I am convinced they cannot have been at it in Shakespeare's day.

It seems to me probable (and here I am aware I am responding subjectively to the scene) that Hamlet continued to hold the skull as the funeral of Ophelia entered the stage. If so, what was the stage-picture? A King and a Queen attended by Lords and a Priest, mourning a corpse (a female suicide, we have already been told), and accompanied by a Young Man in Black. (Laertes' mourning-dress is not specified, but may legitimately be deduced – indeed all the party should at least be wearing black *cloaks*.) By the grave are the Gravediggers, and at a distance stand two other Young Men, one of whom is also in black,* and is holding a Skull. I think he must have been standing slightly angled away from the funeral-party (a convention for 'being unrecognisable'); but he looks at the King; and the King looks at him, and registers a recognition – not of Hamlet as such, but of the clothes and the Skull. Recognition of the *person* is deferred for a few minutes, and then takes the form of an assumption of Kingship by Hamlet: 'This is I, Hamlet the *Dane*.'

Hamlet in this scene, from the King's point of view, is a revenant, a man come back from the dead; and such a grouping as I have suggested is exactly the kind of thing Renaissance painters delighted to present in emblematic memento mori pictures, so popular at the time. (The Murderer confronted by an allegorical figure combining the characteristics of both Victim and Avenger.) We can compare it with the entrance of Brachiano's Ghost in *The White Devil* – a Ghost which not only carries a Skull, in a pot of flowers, but throws earth from the pot towards Flamineo. We can also compare it with the entrance of Giovanni in *'Tis Pity She's A Whore*, where the young man carries the heart of his incestuous sister, whom he has killed, on his dagger – not out of sheer sensationalism, but as a practical demonstration (which is also a moral reflection) of his deed and its significance – the Heart and the Blood would have looked like a religious Sacred Heart Icon, the Dagger piercing the valves of the Heart would have a phallic as well as a lethal appearance. To

* Did Shakespeare intend Horatio to wear black as well? The correct dress of a student would at any rate have been subfusc.

produce the correct hieratic effect of such images, the Actors would have had to avoid all attempt at naturalism, and adopt some formal posture like those of the Kings, Queens and Jacks in a pack of cards with their swords and other properties. If the graveyard scene in *Hamlet* was in fact intended this way, it is not surprising that it has since become an emblem of the whole play : it visually sums up nearly all the main elements of the plot. And carries the plot along – for not until Hamlet meets Laertes can the catastrophe be prepared. It is worth noting, as well, that immediately before the funeral, the audience has *seen* the King and Laertes plotting together, and *heard* them plotting murder. Beside Ophelia's grave the audience thus watches the physical coalescing of all the verbal images of death and corruption that have thronged the dialogue throughout the play.

Let us consider another cluster of visual images in *Hamlet* and their verbal correspondence. The first scene of the play shows the silent visit of a King's Ghost to the sentries on guard at the palace. The stage-directions do not have much to say about the mechanics of this apparition. Merely 'Enter the Ghost', 'Exit the Ghost'; but the comments of the other persons in the scene fill out the picture. He is in armour – and a specific armour – the very suit worn in his lifetime 'When he th' ambitious Norway combated'. This is unusual theatrical practice, indeed probably an innovation. Ghosts normally wore a standard ghost-costume, whatever exactly it may have been, and a realistic earthly dress must have called the audience to pay particular attention. The armour is a complete cap-à-pie outfit, and the Ghost carries a general's truncheon. His walk is a 'solemn march', 'slow and stately'. He goes 'by' the sentries, and when an attempt is made to address him, he 'stalks' away. This dignified, almost arrogant, demeanour, combined with the armour, the truncheon, and the circumstances of the sentry-post suggest a certain type of action, which, if we were not told that the old King was also 'the King that's dead', would be perfectly natural to all concerned. The commander-in-chief is in fact inspecting his guards. I think that, instead of running all over the stage in a panic-stricken way, as I have seen it done in modern productions, Bernardo and

Marcellus – at least during the Ghost's first visit – are supposed to be struck rigid into the normal posture of subordinate soldiers, 'feet together, hands down by the seams of the trousers, eyes facing straight forward . . .' Horatio, the civilian, is the first one to break discipline and speak to the Ghost. The latter has looked his men up and down in the usual way of officers, and then, as though dissatisfied by what he sees, turns on his heel and goes. The second visit, seventy-five lines later, is a more flurried business. The Soldiers aim blows at the Ghost, and it 'fades' – presumably whisking off the stage in a swift pattern of movement that confuses the men and leaves them gasping.

A military apparition – amid military circumstances. The dialogue between the two visits deals with the imminent war with Norway, and Bernardo in fact draws the inference that the Ghost has come to give some sort of warning about this war:

> Well may it sort that this portentous figure
> Comes armed through our watch, so like the king
> That was and is the question of these wars.

Horatio quotes the incidents immediately preceding the Ides of March in Rome; and we are reminded of other theatrical Ghosts of the Elizabethan stage: Caesar's Ghost warning Brutus of the forthcoming battle, the Ghosts of Edward III and the Black Prince in *Woodstock*. There is no reference yet to Claudius or Gertrude or to any of the dynastic troubles within the Danish Royal Family which make up the main plot of the play; and an audience unfamiliar with the story might be led to believe that the play was in fact going to be all about wars between Denmark and Norway and nothing else.

In the next scene we find the King addressing his court: first, briskly enough, on the subject of his marriage, and then – with the air of a man coming to the really important business of the day – he deals with the Norway question and instructs his Ambassadors. Only after they have been dispatched does he attend to Laertes and Hamlet. It is clear that the main preoccupation of this court at this time is the international crisis, which the old King has left as a dangerous legacy to his brother. This part of the scene ends with the King ordering a volley of cannon. Immediately afterwards, Hamlet is told of the Ghost; and in Act I Scene 4 we find him on the platform to see it for himself. While he waits, Claudius's cannon are heard – again impregnating the play with military atmosphere – accompanied by the martial music of kettle drum and trumpet. The Ghost is still in armour; but he does not talk of Norway to his son, only of revenge for a personal wrong. Nevertheless, the conclusion of this scene, with the Dead Old Man in Armour crying bleakly from under the stage, is still reverberant with war-like echoes. Later on in the play there is more talk of Norway – the Ambassadors return in Act II Scene 2, and it seems that the danger has receded. The Ghost in Gertrude's private room (Act III Scene 4) has a different feeling. According to the Quarto text he wears a nightgown, and the personal, sexual atmosphere of the scene relates to the Ghost's *words* in Act I, but by no means to his original appearance.

Act IV scene 3 brings us back again to the wars. Claudius (having – in Act IV Scene 1 – interjected a verbal image of gunfire:

As level as the canon to his blank
Transports his poison'd shot . . .)

– reminds himself of recent successful military action against England: he banks on this to secure English compliance in the death of his nephew. No sooner has Hamlet set out for England than he meets (Act IV Scene 4) 'Fortinbras with an Army'. That is what the Folio stage-direction says: what the audience saw will have been a Living Young Man in Armour, marching at the head of his troops. Could Fortinbras be wearing the same cap-à-pie suit that the Ghost wore in Act I? If so, the only visual difference between Fortinbras and the Ghost is the face revealed by the lifted beaver. Both armoured figures are in the company of soldiers, both of them apparently on military duty. At the very end of the play Fortinbras and his soldiers appear for the last time – with 'March afar off, and shout within', with 'Drum and colours'. Before their entry, while the deadly fencing-match is still in progress, kettledrums are ordered and the stage-direction reads: 'Trumpets sound, and shot goes off'. The last line of the play is 'Go, bid the soldiers shoot.' And the last stage-direction: 'Exeunt marching: after the which a peal of ordnance are shot off.'

In brief: the Dead Old Man in Armour who left the stage in Act I, cried out beneath the stage, and re-entered at the central climax of the play (when Hamlet has actually carried out his mission and killed the King, only it wasn't the King, it was Polonius) as a Dead Old Man dressed for his Wife's Bed, has been seen to come back, rejuvenated, to wind up the whole story, his Norwegian trouble solved, his revenge achieved. Exactly what *interpretation* can be put upon this series of images is not to be argued here. But there can be no doubt that Shakespeare intended his play to be thus framed in warfare and its trappings. *Hamlet* is not just a play about a young man's revenge for the murder of his father and the seduction of his mother. It is a play about the revenge of an heir to the throne *in a nation on a war-footing*: and the most vivid indication that this is so is provided by the stagecraft rather than the speeches.

When talking about stagecraft, we must not forget that sound effects are as important as visual demonstrations. We have already noted how the cannon and military music recur throughout the play. There is another *Hamlet* episode in which music is crucial to the full understanding of the Playwright's intention: Act III Scene 1, the play-within-the-play, the second basic confrontation between Hamlet and Claudius. (The first is in Act I Scene 2, when Claudius speaks from the throne, and Hamlet hovers edgily on the sidelines. In the play-scene Hamlet begins with a similar sideline business, but ends by defying the King to his face, to some extent an oblique defiance, even yet, expressed 'tropically'. The defiance is continued into the third confrontation, Act IV Scene 3, after the death of Polonius. But here Hamlet has had to be fetched by force, and is at a disadvantage. The fourth confrontation is at the graveside – Hamlet displays to Claudius the *physical* image of revenge and death. And finally, at the fencing-match, the fifth confrontation: revenge and death themselves.) Apart from the obvious narrative of the play-scene, what stagecraft does Shakespeare employ to mark the crucial moment of the second confrontation? The King's entrance is noted thus:

Enter King, Queen, Polonius, Ophelia, Rosencrantz, Guildenstern, and other lords attendant with his guard carrying torches. Danish march. Sound a flourish.

The Danish march involved the kettledrums, a fairly thunderous affair, bringing us once again the established military and alcoholic flavour of King Claudius. As soon as the play begins, however, a different music is heard. 'Hoboyes play': wood-wind. This is not only the Players' music, but – by association – Hamlet's. After the King has left the stage, taking his soldiers and torches with him, Hamlet calls for music: and he calls for wood-wind. A recorder is physically delivered: it is not said to be played, but I suspect that 'Look you, these are the stops' might be intended as a cue for Hamlet to blow a few notes. At all events, he then goes on to draw a verbal analogy between the pipe and the situation. The visual and aural contrast of the two musics in this scene reflects the threefold contrast between Hamlet, his warlike father, and his apparently warlike but in fact diplomatic uncle – an essential theme of the play, picked up again visually in the Queen's chamber when Hamlet will be seen standing between the portraits of old Hamlet and Claudius, confronting the woman who has slept with two of these three men and been brought to bed of the third.

It will have been noted that the imagery of the stagecraft in *Hamlet* does not contradict its verbal counterpoint. It amplifies, fulfils and to some extent provides a large new dimension to the narrative as stated in the speeches. But in another play, *Henry V*, there is a remarkable and consistent disparity between what is said to be done and what is seen to be done. Peter Brook's remarks, quoted at the head of this essay, on the subject of the 'secret play' within the intellectually apparent surface-play, are pertinent here: though Brook's meaning is not quite my meaning. He seems to have been looking for a series of more or less *subconscious* themes underlying the overt plot (rather as when a man is told 'You do look well today', he might understand the greeting to mean not only what it says but also 'You are not at all well, in fact, but your jealousy of me compels you to an excessive brightness' – yet the brightness is so well assumed, the original remark must none the less be taken as a sincere and accurate assessment of the man's demeanour). In *Henry V* on the other hand, I believe the 'secret play' is a *deliberate* attempt by Shakespeare to contradict his overt play for political reasons.

Henry V had already been treated in the theatre and his story had become an historical cliché. The victory of Agincourt was a classical pretext for jingoistic demonstrations that one Englishman was worth ten Frenchmen, that no Continental power should dare to adopt policies which offended the rights of the patriotic islanders, that England in the sixteenth century had discovered a national identity far stronger and more virtuous than that of any other nation. Shakespeare had already worked his way through the reigns of Richard II and Henry IV, and his argument was leading him inevitably to the orthodox conclusions about Henry V. A self-indulgent king (Richard) had allowed his country to sink into such chaos that only through the sacrilegious deposition and murder of the monarch could any solution be found; but this sacrilege carried with it an inherent curse, of which the rebellions in the next reign and the debaucheries of the heir to the throne were to be the chronic symptoms. In the end the reformed Prince Hal must come to power and purge the dynasty by the justice and splendour of his reign. He was to be the ideal type of national Christian monarch, untainted by his father's guilt, having cast off by his own will-power all those elements in his character that resembled King Richard's folly. Now this character had to be built up through the course of both parts of *Henry IV*, and already, as he prepares this work, Shakespeare becomes conscious of a certain moral equivocation.

If Hal is really to reform, he cannot be shown to be completely seduced by the grossness of the Falstaff gang, so he has to be made aware of his future transformation at a sufficiently early stage.

> I know you all, and will awhile uphold
> The unyok'd humour of your idleness ...
> My reformation, glittering o'er my fault,
> Shall show more goodly and attract more eyes
> Than that which hath no foil to set it off.
> I'll so offend to make offence a skill;
> Redeeming time when men think least I will.

This speech, right at the beginning of *Henry IV Part I*, has a most unpleasant ring about it – a calculating, play-acting, political chancer's confession, and there can be no accident about it. Shakespeare had the alternative of portraying Hal as a genuinely confused, lusty Juventus, drawn despite himself to carnal vice, and earnestly seeking his spiritual deliverance. This alternative was rejected: we cannot know why, but I think Shakespeare had come to realise that successful hereditary politicians are taught calculation and opportunism from the cradle. A Plantagenet born into a housefull of scheming Plantagenets could never have responded naturally to lust or emotion or affection or remorse – or, if he could, he would grow up to be more like Henry VI – which was not what was to happen. But if this chilling creature was really to be turned into the beloved Harry of the next play but one, was not the entire moral framework of the tetralogy about to be reduced to a brutal Machiavellian tract stating simply 'When the kingdom is fraught with internal conflict, the easiest way out is a victorious foreign war' ...?

It is surely apparent from everything Shakespeare ever wrote that he could not have accepted this as a desirable doctrine. We must be careful not to attribute to a sixteenth-century writer any modish anti-imperialism; but conquest and bloodshed have been hated by true poets since the time of Homer, and I cannot believe that Shakespeare could have happily sat down to elevate them into a criterion of beneficent rule. On the other hand, he had begun his epic cycle, and it was proving popular on the stage. The acting-company naturally wanted it to be completed, and the public were expectant. If *Henry V* turned out to be an exercise in cynical debunking, the patriotic passions of the audience would be seriously disappointed, and in all likelihood the play would be hissed. Shakespeare was not writing for a sophisticated élite – *Henry V* must be for the public theatre or nowhere. But suppose the play were *not* hissed: suppose that a debunking treatment of the Agincourt campaign were in fact to strike a nerve of serious disillusion with official politics, and people were to flock to the playhouse in order to *applaud* the actors who condemned the personification of England's past greatness and future unity? Queen Elizabeth's reign, in its last years, was not happy – the glorious deliverance from the Spanish Armada had not brought about economic prosperity and content for all classes. More importantly, the Irish were in a state of serious hostility.

Any play on a national theme put on at this time would have to take account of the Irish wars, which are far from glorious. There is indeed a dedication in *Henry V* to the Earl of Essex as he assumed his Irish command. We do not need the present carnage in Ulster to remind us that the one place where English armies have *never* obtained glory is Ireland. Essex, in the outcome, was to be baffled by a guerilla force of bare-legged wood-kerne, and driven to a treaty: it took all the intense frightfulness of Mountjoy's later campaign to 'finally' settle the Irish. There were enough old soldiers around the London taprooms to have given Shakespeare more than an inkling of this, even before Essex took ship. An intelligent Playwright with political sensitivity could only connect an expedition to Ireland with bloody waste at best and naked cruelty at worst. And if that same Playwright found it needful to connect it also with the historic expedition of his alleged hero-king, then it was obvious he was treading very delicate ground.

An overt attack upon Henry's character would be taken by many as an attack on Essex, the Queen's favourite (and a close friend of the Poet's patron) – or even as an attack upon the Queen herself. That class of suspicion did not merely mean bad news at the box-office. It brought actual danger of imprisonment and torture to the theatre-company who invited it. Ben Jonson was to be branded and twice imprisoned for the implications of his work: Kyd was racked: and Marlowe was only saved from a police investigation by his sudden death. Today (1976) at a time of terrorism and counter-terrorism, industrial militance, and overdone obsessions with 'security', Playwrights are not immune from such considerations. The usual sanction in Britain now is financial (though in other parts of the world Writers have been on trial for their lives); and a recent issue of the London *'Workers' Press'* (9 February, 1976) contains the following item:

*Union play under attack.* The right wing is attacking a play about militant trade unionism that received a £16,000 Arts Council grant. The play, called *The Nine Days and Saltley Gates*, is performed by the group Foco Novo. Nicholas Fairbairn, the Tory MP for Kinross and West Perthshire, says the production is an incitement to industrial disruption.

An Arts Council Grant today, though to some extent a protection, is looked upon by many politicians with a very dubious eye. The Lord Chamberlain's patronage of Elizabethan Actors who did not toe the line over historic English foreign policy must have undergone the same scrutiny. When the chips are down neither Arts Council officials nor the Lord Chamberlain could be expected to shelter a Playwright at the expense of their careers ...

Shakespeare seems to have decided that he could not risk an outright continuation of Hal's shifty character from *Henry IV*. If he wanted to debunk warrior-heroes, the play to do it in would be *Troilus and Cressida*: no one in Westminster politics cared a rap about Troy. But he would not 'change sides' over his view of King Henry. Instead he would prepare an overt text and a secret play in parallel – the one would be for the jingoes and the common-informers: the other for people who thought as he did but could not safely say so. The result is a published text, which, if curtailed, and edited out of its original scene-order, need show no trace of the Author's dual structure. Laurence Olivier's famous film, made during the Second World War as a patriotic clarion-call to a democracy fighting dictatorship, was a grand and simple glorification

of a small army confronted by enormous odds. Not only did
Olivier remove all suggestion of Henry's moral deviousness, but he
also softened the arrogance which had been designed to prove the
Poet's orthodoxy to the original audience. He was able to do this
because Shakespeare allowed the strength of his rhetorical skill full
scope in the dialogue: there is no snide undermining of the sense
of the speeches by ambiguous diction. Henry speaks, in public, as
the ideal of Christian chivalry ought to have spoken; and the Chorus
(conventionally the Dramatist's own voice, and therefore *to be
trusted* by the audience, if the audience is not wise to what is
happening) declaims the acceptable, expected sentiments with
abounding sincerity. But what is seen to take place around these
great set-pieces is the clue to the 'secret play'. A number of examples
should demonstrate clearly enough the validity of my argument.

In the first scene of the play two Bishops discuss the activities of
the new King, and express alarm about Parliamentary proposals
to levy exactions upon the Church. In order to influence the King
against these, they have determined to press the legitimacy of his
title to the French crown. Henry gives audience to the ecclesiastics
before he sees the French Ambassador. He demands a conscientious
legal justification for his French claim, which is given him – at
length – by the Archbishop of Canterbury. The care with which
the King invokes 'right and conscience' and the inordinate detail
of Canterbury's historical exegesis occupy no fewer than ninety-
five lines of Act I Scene 2. The scene, so far, impresses the audience
with the King's reluctance to indulge in military adventure for its
own sake. But under all the morality of government, it has also
become clear, to those who pay close attention, that a plan has been
carefully made to divide the available English force so that the
expedition can be properly supported and its base protected from
the north. In other words, the war is already planned; and all that
is needed is the King's final decision, which he makes (line 221),
'Now are we well resolved', immediately before the Ambassadors of
France come in. When they come in, they prove to bring an insult-
ing message *in reply* to a demand previously made by Henry to the
French crown for certain dukedoms. This is the first we have heard

of this demand. Henry, in fact, has *not* waited for his conscience to be satisfied before issuing ultimata to France – and only the length of the first part of Scene 2 prevents the audience from grasping this. Shakespeare here is using the lay-out of his stage-groupings (first the Bishops alone, then the King and Nobles and Bishops together, then the whole court plus Ambassadors) to display and conceal at one and the same time the duplicity of Henry's politics.

The Ambassadors offer him tennis-balls. Henry replies in a long angry speech (37 lines), which concludes with a fierce declaration of *vengeance*. He presents his already planned war to the French diplomats *apparently as a result* of the tennis-ball insult. Adult schoolboys in the audience will notice nothing odd: but persons with an eye to the Bishops still standing behind the King will remember and take note of what those Bishops have already devised.

Act II begins with the Chorus, who invokes a passionate feeling of 'all the youth of England ... on fire'. But by the time we get to the end of Act II Scene 3, the play is nearly one-third over, and what have we actually *seen* of the English public to justify the high-sounding terms of Chorus? A group of Nobles, nearly all of them the King's close relatives; a pair of Prelates concerned to secure their revenues from secular confiscation; a sample of the London criminal classes; three aristocratic conspirators, hired by the French to kill the King in the name of an English dynastic quarrel; and we have also been told of a man who 'railed at' the King while drunk. The Pistol crowd have been allotted two scenes in one act, and in the second one their views on the honourable war are unequivocal:

Let us to France; like horse-leeches, my boys,
To suck, to suck, the very blood to suck!

It has needed the most expert deployment of blank verse by the Chorus and the King to cover over the implications of these tableaux. Yet, somehow, when the Army goes to France, it does seem to go as a fellowship of 'dear countrymen' under 'the hand of God'. We have not been *shown* how this can be, and Shakespeare is well aware he has not shown it. There would have been no difficulty for him to have given at least one picture of honest enthusiastic volunteers setting forth to achieve the Kings' Right: that he does not do so can only be by deliberate choice.

The great Harfleur speech 'Once more unto the breach, dear friends' is so well-known and so perennially effective in the theatre that (as with many great speeches in this play) the fervour of its delivery tends to muffle what is actually seen to be happening on the stage. Who responds to it? It is heard, according to the Folio stage-direction, only by Exeter, Bedford, and Gloucester (together with some unnamed men carrying scaling-ladders, who have no lines). The named Nobles are the King's uncle and his two brothers, whose family interests are directly benefited by the war, and at risk if it is lost. When Henry finishes, the men who are seen to be attacking the breach – or rather, failing yet again to attack the breach – are Pistol, Bardolph, Nym, and their Boy. They must be driven to the assault by Fluellen, so little has the King's oratory fired them. The Boy, left behind, comments on their skrimshanking. Then there is the scene with the four Captains. This is the first scene in the whole play which suggests that the English Army has any sort of professional expertise in its ranks. As only one of the four is an Englishman, we conclude that the expertise is largely made up from mercenary sources. The mood of these seasoned men is gloomy: MacMorris is disgusted with the command-decisions about his land-mines, and Fluellen is disgusted with the incompetence of MacMorris. It is thus quietly suggested that the most reliable part of the Army is demoralised and badly led ...

Shakespeare's technique in this play will by now have become clear. He regularly sets up a certain atmosphere of noble enterprise by means of evocative blank verse speeches, and without comment, deflates it through an alternation of scenes showing something very near the opposite. 'A little touch of Harry in the night' is a line which so sums up the devoted commander among his troops that it has become a positive cliché. Nelson, for instance, was inspired by it. But again, it is only what we are *told* about Harry, not quite what we are to *see*. What we do see is positively the first appearance in the play of representative respectable private-soldiers: and they

are despondent. Michael Williams accuses the King of having led
them all to death for a cause they know nothing of. Henry engages
him in low-toned prose argument about obedience and the moral
responsibility of those who give orders and those who receive them;
but he does not answer the main point at issue which can be nothing
other than 'What right has the King to drag us all into this disaster?'
Williams regards his probable death the next morning without
lightness of heart: and his anger is deeply-felt. Against whom
does he feel it? The King is in disguise, but his manner is of the
officers' mess. One must suppose the Soldiers take him for some
tiresome young nosey-parker interfering where he is not wanted
with ill-considered propaganda on behalf of the Staff. 'A little touch
of Harry' is a meaningless remark if what the men are actually
seen to receive is a little touch of an uncertain anonymous subaltern,
who only succeeds in getting their backs up. The King's disguised
prowl, in fact, has not been for the purpose of heartening the
Soldiers at all. He merely wanted to spy on them . . . He has a
soliloquy: he complains in fifty-four lines of verse that it is not fair
for everyone to blame the King for the war which the King has
organised, when all that the King has endeavoured to do has been
to 'maintain the peace'. His subsequent prayer is of the nature of a
quid pro quo with God. But its crude materialism has been carefully
modified by the Erpingham conversation – the gallant pathos of this
old knight frames the scene at beginning and end, and provides the
overriding poetic tone, which is not absolutely smothered by the
other matter. Out of the whole Army, Sir Thomas Erpingham is
the only man *shown* who is in fact moved by the 'touch of Harry
in the night'.

The order of scenes during the battle is not without significance.
After the King's noble rebuff to the French Herald, events are
presented thus:

(a) *Pistol* extorts a ransom from a terrified Frenchman (cf. 'come
thou no more for ransom, gentle herald').

(b) Pistol's Boy remarks that the baggage has only himself and his
fellow-juveniles to guard it.

(c) The French General Staff are confounded by their sudden reverse.

(d) 'Enter the King and his train, with Prisoners'. The battle appears to be won.

(e) 'The French have reinforced their scattered men'. The King briskly gives order that every man must kill his prisoners.

(f) Fluellen and Gower lament the murder of the boys on the baggage-guard, by 'the cowardly rascals that ran from the battle'. Gower explains that the order to kill the prisoners is the direct result of this atrocity.

(g) Fluellen tells how Alexander the Great once killed his best friend.

(h) 'Enter King Harry and Bourbon with Prisoners'. The King displays anger, no doubt at the murder of the boys, though he does not say so. He then *threatens* to kill his prisoners if the remaining French do not surrender or 'void the field'. Mountjoy concedes defeat, asking for a chance to bury the French dead.

(i) The King derives a lengthy comic plot from the challenge-glove he exchanged with Williams the previous night.

(j) The casualty list, for which the King has been waiting throughout episode (i) arrives. The enormous number of French dead and the miraculous sparing of English lives leads into a sober threnody by the King, giving all the credit to God; and they march out, perhaps actually singing 'Non Nobis and Te Deum'.

Now, how can the Prisoners – ordered to be slain in episode (e), and presumably *seen* hauled out to their deaths – revive and be brought in again in episode (h)? Were they killed or weren't they? And if they were, for what cause? Henry says they must die because the French reinforcements have arrived – i.e. if the English are to fight a still vigorous remainder of the Constable's force, there is a danger that their captives must be left in the rear without a proper guard, and they may be able to attack their exhausted captors from behind. This would be a sound military reason: if a repellent one. It is *not* given in the text, in so many words. If, on the other hand, they are to be killed because the boys have been murdered, the emotional force behind the reprisal will be recognised: but the deed would hardly be accepted as chivalrous. Gower, as a simple soldier with no inclination towards moral scrupulosities, assumes the second reason to be the right one, and approves it. (In Olivier's film, by the way, the French atrocity was emphasised by the actual sight of a murdered boy: while the English atrocity was omitted altogether.) The second arrival on stage of a group of Prisoners might suggest that the King's order has not been obeyed. But Gower and Fluellen have already implied that it was obeyed. So this must be a *second* batch of Prisoners, taken no doubt from the French reinforcements. The King, therefore, seeing that there are still a few French remaining in the field, secures their final surrender by threatening a *second massacre*. This is the clear sense of the passage, combining the speeches with the stage-directions: and, taken at face value, it gives the King's behaviour a flavour of savage ferocity. The very confusion in the heat of battle-excitement about which Prisoners are killed, and why, and when (indeed, if any are killed) does however act as a sort of alibi. It would be hard for an audience coming out of the theatre to take oath as to exactly what *has* happened in this part of the story; and those who would dislike the idea of Harry as a murderer of surrendered men can easily enough give him the benefit of the doubt and assume that in fact all the prisoners were spared. Not every one would dislike this idea, though. Queen Elizabeth had been pleased to congratulate her commander at Smerwick in Ireland when he put to the sword a surrendered garrison. But then, as ever, certain double standards applied to Irish operations ... it is possible that the Alexander-Cleitus reference is intended not only to echo the casting-off of Falstaff but also – subliminally – to place in our minds the picture of a great conqueror who behaved at least once in an atrocious way. But it is passed over so rapidly in the action that one cannot be sure of this.

Could the whole problem conceivably be a mare's-nest; the contradictory references to, and visual displays of Prisoners no more than errors in the copying of the prompt-scripts? If there had been no other ambiguities throughout the play, this would be the most likely explanation; but the killing of the Prisoners is a black spot on the King's reputation, and Shakespeare could have missed it out completely, like Olivier, had he wished. He could also have emphasised it and condemned it. Either way, the script would have been clear. As it is, he takes a third course – he shows it, through conscious dramatic muddle, as a part-justified, part-unmotivated moment of horror, which the discerning can think about and the careless will ignore.

Immediately afterwards the audience has the uncomplicated humour of Williams and his quarrel to divert their attention* – they are all however recalled to the reality of slaughter when the casualty-lists are brought in. By this time the tone is back again at the melancholy solemnity of the end of Act IV Scene 1 ('Not today, O Lord! O not today, think not upon the fault my father made in compassing the crown, etc . . .') and religious music brings the whole battle-sequence to an end.

Between the scenes, before Act V Scene 2, Henry has made certain political demands of the defeated French King, which a council must discuss and ratify before a treaty can be concluded. It then appears that while this conference is taking place (off-stage) Henry will propose marriage to the Princess. If she refuses, his boyish affection leads us to believe, he will be deeply disappointed: but the other parts of the treaty, once agreed upon, will stand. The amount of text devoted (a) to the territorial demands before the couple are left alone (26 lines), and (b) to the amorous duologue (206 lines) acts as a smokescreen to conceal the two crucial lines of King Henry:

> She is our capital demand, compris'd
> Within the fore-rank of our articles.

The French King has his doubts about some of the territorial demands. He temporises:

* The original argument that led to the quarrel is conveniently forgotten – though Shakespeare surely expected some of the audience to remember it.

I have but with a cursorary eye
O'er-glanc'd the articles . . .

– and on his return from the conference there is still one item to be
finally settled. This is not the marriage of his daughter, however,
which is stated by Westmorland at this juncture to be definitely
agreed upon: the success of Henry's wooing only needs to be *confirmed* by the bride's father. But in fact there can have been *no*
haggling in the off-stage council about the Princess. The very circumstances that she has been left alone with Henry proves that the
French King has no objection to the match, but is happy to indulge
the young couple with a pretence that their love-making is entirely
independent of political necessity. From the very beginning of the
scene, Kate knows, and Henry knows, that the marriage must take
place. The sentiment between the two of them therefore is all play-
acting: she is making the best of it, and he is presenting himself as
usual in the most attractive possible image. None of this is immediately apparent from the verbal text on its own – it is the sandwich-
ing of the lovers' duologue between two full court-scenes which
reveals the full state of affairs; and to understand it requires the
ability to look at the complete structure of a play before and behind
the scene actually on the stage. The irony is implicit in the *action*,
and therefore can easily be missed, if only the spoken text is regarded. And to think of Act V Scene 2 as a *love-scene* is in itself mis-
leading. It is really a scene of political settlement in which the
forced amity of conquered towards conqueror is illustrated by two
passages of regal pleasantry separated by a sexual play-within-the-
play – an emblem of a cease-fire which lasted historically for a very
short time. Members of the audience who had seen *Henry VI Part 1*
would well realise just how short.

To sum up – the overall message of *Henry V*, derived not only
from the rhetoric but also from the stagecraft of the play, may
approximately be read: 'By all realistic political criteria, Henry
V is agreed to have been the most successful and desirable national
leader who emerged from the Plantagenet squabbles of the early
fifteenth century. We need, and perhaps have got, such leadership

today. But take him as a human being, made by and making history, and assess him at his real worth – do you like what you see? If not, what can be done about it?' The deeds of England's Harry make a very pessimistic play indeed ...

These detailed investigations into the dual structure of *Hamlet* and *Henry V* are intended less as a contribution to Shakespearian scholarship than as a means of identifying the use that a Dramatist (justly celebrated for his *words*) could also make of the three-dimensional technicalities of the stage – *without* the assistance of a Director to interpret his play for him. Of course any production of Shakespeare today requires a Director. I have here been concerned only with the plays when they were new, as unknown to the Actors as they were to the Audience, and with only two weeks or so to worry them into meaningful shape. Any play of quality is expected to present a characteristic vision of the world. It is assumed that this will be the personal vision of the Dramatist – unless the company presenting the play is a truly collaborative collective (in which case the vision is communal, and therefore inevitably to an extent generalised – usually such work will adopt some recognised political, religious, or social doctrine already familiar to devotees and available in books like the Bible or the writings of Marx). But if the Dramatist believes that the text is only the jumping-off point for the far more complete and *theatrical* art of the Director and the Acting-company, and if he or she makes all the statements in terms of dialogue, leaving the stage-craft to the others, then the vision must needs become adulterated before it can be passed on to the Audience.

It may be that the Playwright and the Director and everyone else will find themselves sharing the same point of view, and thereby a kind of joint commitment will obtain; but the structure of theatre in contemporary Western Society affords no guarantee of such ideological harmony. Even if the Company is formally committed to, say, Socialist principles – as so many groups now claim – the multitudes of sects and heresies which entangle the left wing of a monopoly-capitalist culture are bound sooner or later to intrude their divisions. The Playwright for such a Company, excluded as is so often the case from the day-to-day control of rehearsals, may well be set at odds with the ideological consensus among the Actors, whose opinions are more likely to be influenced by the Director than the Author. The latter's play, developed in private, will prove, when presented to the Company, out of line with their policy, and will either not be performed, or will be so altered that the writer's personal statement will practically cease to exist.

Now plays written to a received doctrinal formula do not, in the long run, enhance the art of theatre. I believe that one of the main qualities of this art is its capacity for continual and fruitful criticism of received ideas, *particularly* those ideas which the Playwright holds most dear. But a Playwright who is not regarded as the primary source for all the ideas (whether explicit through the spoken word or implicit in the stagecraft) which the play transmits, becomes by degrees crippled in capacity for expression. The theatre does not exist to *interpret* plays, but to *present* them. It is a truism that the play-script on the page is not the complete work of art – only when it is performed and the necessary two-way communication between Actors and Audience has taken place, can the Drama in the fullest sense be said to have been created.

If we still believe that the vision of the individual artist has any importance in our society, then that artist, as Playwright, must clearly be in control of his or her work right through to the final exit of the Audience from their seats in the theatre. But, to claim such control, such an artist must be able to understand the principles of all the work done by all the other members of the Company. In the present state of affairs few are capable of this. The Director, of course, does make such a claim. But it is a false one. For there is one crucial part of the Company's work which Directors can rarely do (or else they would not be known as 'Directors') – and that is to write the plays. They often *create performances*, without writers; and thereby produce the kind of diluted theatrical esperanto which I have described in the first part of this essay. But in general they adopt the attitude that the Playwright is *outside* the Company, and should not be encouraged *into* it, because the Director and the Director alone can 'deal with Actors'. If this is true, it is because Playwrights have no training and experience at dealing with Actors. (Or, to put it another way, Directors have no training and experience at writing plays.)

I received a letter recently from a student of 'Theatre Studies' at a British University. She described her course as one 'designed to show the problems of actors and directors, but particularly it outlines the struggle for survival of Theatre in today's society'. Not a mention of Playwrights. Theatre, in a contemporary academic environment, is thus regarded as the preserve of those who have been sealed off by contemporary theatrical practice into the ghetto of *performance*. The other ghetto, script-writing, is well away across the tracks, sharing its cabins with the practitioners of *literature*. Is it any wonder that this University has its doubts about the *survival* of the art?

Playwriting, of course, is literature, insofar as plays can be read in private and – up to a point – enjoyed for their words' sake. But surely it is time that the great gulf between the craft of the Novelist or Lyric Poet and the craft of the Dramatist could once again be recognised, as it was in the sixteenth century? There will always be a place in the theatre for Novelists and Poets who have happened to write a good play, but who do not feel capable of presenting it on the stage. The work of such artists will need a Director. But they must be thought of as *Play-writers*, not *Playwrights*. Is it necessary to explain that these two terms, although they sound rather alike, are etymologically quite distinct? A Play-writer is simply a person who puts pen to paper and sets down dramatic dialogue. But the Playwright pursues an ancient and complex craft analogous to the crafts of the Cartwright, the Millwright, the Shipwright, or – in old Scots – the Wright, pure and simple. The origin of the word is Old English *Wyrht* = a work, or *Wyrcan* = to work. The Playwright *works* drama just as the Millwright *works* mill-gear. And working or making a play includes what are now thought to be the activities of the Director *as well as* those of the Script-writer. Such an artist requires a wider workshop than the keyboard of a typewriter. He/she must see him/herself as a person capable of presenting a complete artistic vision upon the stage – not as a semiskilled sub-contractor to the theatre, who requires someone else actually to produce the play once its text is completed. At times, of course, a particular skill in the arranging of the stage-spectacle may be called for, and it may be convenient for a Director to assist the Playwright in this. But there is a lot of difference between an assistant and an overall artistic governor.

I should at this point make it clear that I am talking about the first production of a new play only. Obviously – in a world where plays are translated into many languages and presented in their original language by many widely-spaced Companies (as was not the case with the Elizabethans) – Directors will be required for all productions at which the Playwright cannot personally be present. If the result of the first performance is, as it should be, a published text incorporating all the modifications arrived at during rehearsals, the amount of 'creative variation' available to other theatres will not be very great. But the Playwright, at, in, and throughout the first production seems to me an absolute essential. To achieve this there is no doubt that the entire system of training Actors, employing Writers, and administering theatres will need to be changed. The training of Playwrights will also have to be undertaken. Not, I hasten to add, in Universities. Practical professional apprenticeship is called for, and this would involve the learning of the techniques of acting, scene-designing, basic musical skills, et cetera.

I had few of these skills myself. I joined a profession crippled by generations of exclusion from the workshop-floor – and I found it a grave hindrance at all stages of my career as a Playwright. However, after twenty-two years of active participation in theatrical work, I am now bold enough to claim that I have more experience, knowledge and general skill than a large number of the Directors currently earning money as experts in the trade – experts in every branch of it except my own, that is.

I really do not know how all this can be attained, short of the right sort of political and social revolution; but the most helpful departure would seem to be through the activities of the trade-union. Playwrights regard themselves generally as unsuitable subjects for militant organisation. But this is only because their professional crippling has taken the form of an emphasis on their individual separation from the body of their fellow-workers in the theatrical craft. Once Dramatists can see themselves as essential and permanent members of the Acting-companies, they will also be able to see themselves as wrongfully excluded therefrom by the development of the current system, and thus they will be led to organise themselves with their colleagues to recapture their looted rights. We must be humble, and we must be arrogant. Admit that we don't know all the aspects of our job as well as we might: and demand that we be granted the opportunity to master them. Hitherto, Playwrights' Unions have concentrated upon the improvement of the working conditions and remuneration of their members within the existing structure. This will not do any more. The structure – with all its political and financial and artistic implications – must be challenged: or our craft will die.

*Epilogue*

# Epilogue

Some readers may well wonder why I have been harping so much upon what they perhaps regard as 'a passing phase' in Anglo-Irish relationships: what has all this tedious political history really got to do with the 'ancient principles of theatre' the man talks about on his first page? Not necessarily anything: except that I live in Ireland, and therefore its affairs must in some sort be *my* affairs. The quickest way for a playwright to be absorbed without trace into the meaningless foam-rubber of the jumbo-jet culture (see page 177) is to ignore the public life of the region where he lives. Ireland, for me, now, is Pieter Bruegel's crowded market-place. It is also, as it happens, and for reasons I have already given, a most significant corner of the entire British theatre's market-place: but a corner screened-off by a blanket of wilful ignorance and left to fester unvisited and (as is hoped) unobserved.

A gentleman from the National Theatre in London told me recently that he regarded himself as 'a revolutionary', and that he intended, by working gradually within that prestigious* organisation, to ensure that the repertoire included as many plays as possible upon strong social, political, relevant revolutionary themes. Not long after this conversation, the NT Script Department had occasion to request the return of a book they had lent me, and they courteously sent me postage-stamps to cover the cost of despatching it. The letter enclosing the stamps was supplied with a printed

* *Prestigious.* Common contemporary vernacular meaning = *possessing prestige.* Correct dictionary definition = *juggling, deceitful.*

heading: 'NATIONAL THEATRE ... patron H.M. The Queen'. Each of the enclosed postage-stamps bore a profile portrait of Her Majesty ... I replied with thanks and an expression of regret that I had not been able to use them 'because the Irish Republic has its own postal system'. Such acute political awareness of the potential subject-matter of late-twentieth-century English-speaking playwrights in the new South Bank temple to the art of Shakespeare and Jonson, O'Casey, Synge, Shaw, Beckett, surely speaks for itself.

I say no more: I have no more to say.
I now propose to start a brand-new play.

1976